Que® Quick Reference Series

AutoCAD Quick Reference

Brenda L. Fouch

Que Corporation
Carmel, Indiana

Library of Congress Catalog Number: 89-60197

ISBN 0-88022-425-8

92 91 90 89   4 3 2 1

Interpretation of the printing code: the rightmost double-
digit number is the year of the book's printing; the
rightmost single-digit number, the number of the book's
printing. For example, a printing code of 89-4 shows
that the fourth printing of the book occurred in 1989.

Information in this book is based on AutoCAD Release
10. Commands and functions detailed in this book
should work with other releases in which the pertinent
features are available.

Que Quick Reference Series

The *Que Quick Reference Series* is a portable resource of essential microcomputer knowledge. Whether you are a new or experienced user, you can rely on the high-quality information contained in these convenient guides.

Drawing on the experience of many of Que's best-selling authors, the *Que Quick Reference Series* helps you easily access important program information. Now it's easy to look up programming information for assembly language, C, QuickBASIC 4, and Turbo Pascal as well as often-used commands and functions for 1-2-3, WordPerfect 5, MS-DOS, dBASE IV, and AutoCAD.

Use the *Que Quick Reference Series* as a compact alternative to confusing and complicated traditional documentation.

The *Que Quick Reference Series* also includes these titles:

> *Assembly Language Quick Reference*
> *DOS and BIOS Functions Quick Reference*
> *C Quick Reference*
> *QuickBASIC Quick Reference*
> *Turbo Pascal Quick Reference*
> *1-2-3 Quick Reference*
> *dBASE IV Quick Reference*
> *Hard Disk Quick Reference*
> *MS-DOS Quick Reference*
> *WordPerfect Quick Reference*

Publishing Manager
   Allen L. Wyatt, Sr.

Editors
   Gail S. Burlakoff
   Gregory Croy
   Rebecca Whitney

Editorial Assistant
   Ann K. Taylor

Table of Contents

FUNCTION KEYS

F1 = GRAPHICS MODE TO TEXT MODE
       TEXT MODE TO GRAPHICS MODE

F6 = STATIC MEASUREMENTS ON
          STATUS LINE
          TOGGLE
       SCROLLING MEASUREMENTS ON
          STATUS LINE

F7 = TOGGLE GRID ON/OFF

F8 = TOGGLE ORTHO MODE ON/OFF

F9 = TOGGLE SNAP MODE ON/OFF

F10 = TABLET OFF

Introduction

This command reference is meant to serve as a quick guide for new and experienced users alike. It covers the commands and functions used within AutoCAD; it does not cover concepts that may be essential to effective use of the program. For that type of information, you should refer to a full-featured tutorial book such as *Using AutoCAD*, published by Que Corporation.

This book is divided into two parts. The first part provides a purpose, syntax, and description for each command. The second part is a table with an emphasis on the various selections at command prompts. Some commands used in programming are included in this reference for the sake of defining commands for new users.

Throughout this book, information shown in a different typeface (such as Command:) is generally a prompt used by AutoCAD. Information you would enter is shown in uppercase bold type (such as **APERTURE**).

Please note that some commands, such as ZOOM and PAN, may be used within other commands. These commands are presented in their internal use form—that is, preceded by an apostrophe. The apostrophe is not necessary when the command is being used at the AutoCAD Command: prompt.

AutoCAD Commands

The following is a list of AutoCAD commands (including dimensioning commands) in alphabetical order. Each command is covered within this quick reference, beginning immediately after the list.

ALIGNED	AREA
ANGULAR	ARRAY
APERTURE	ATTDEF
ARC	ATTDISP

ATTEDIT
ATTEXT
AXIS
BASE
BASELINE
BLIPMODE
BLOCK
BREAK
CENTER
CHAMFER
CHANGE
CHPROP
CIRCLE
COLOR
CONTINUE
COPY
DBLIST
DDATTE
'DDEMODES
'DDLMODES
'DDRMODES
DDUCS
DELAY
DIAMETER
DIM or DIM1
DIST
DIVIDE
DONUT
   or DOUGHNUT
DRAGMODE
DTEXT
DVIEW
DXBIN
DXFIN
DXFOUT
EDGESURF
ELEV

ELLIPSE
END
ERASE
EXIT
EXPLODE
EXTEND
FILES
FILL
FILLET
FILMROLL
'GRAPHSCR
GRID
HANDLES
HATCH
'HELP or '?
HIDE
HOMETEXT
HORIZONTAL
ID
IGESIN
IGESOUT
INSERT
ISOPLANE
LAYER
LEADER
LIMITS
LINE
LINETYPE
LIST
LOAD
LTSCALE
MEASURE
MENU
MINSERT
MIRROR
MOVE
MSLIDE

MULTIPLE	'SETVAR
NEWTEXT	SH
OFFSET	SHAPE
OOPS	SHELL
ORTHO	SKETCH
OSNAP	SNAP
'PAN	SOLID
PEDIT	STATUS
PLAN	STRETCH
PLINE	STYLE
PLOT	TABLET
POINT	TABSURF
POLYGON	TEXT
PRPLOT	'TEXTSCR
PURGE	TIME
QTEXT	TRACE
QUIT	TRIM
RADIUS	U
REDEFINE	UCS
REDO	UCSICON
'REDRAW	UNDEFINE
'REDRAWALL	UNDO
REGEN	UNITS
REGENALL	UPDATE
REGENAUTO	VERTICAL
RENAME	'VIEW
'RESUME	VIEWPORTS or
REVSURF	VPORTS
ROTATE	VIEWRES
ROTATED	VPOINT
RSCRIPT	VSLIDE
RULESURF	WBLOCK
SAVE	'ZOOM
SCALE	3DFACE
SCRIPT	3DMESH
SELECT	3DPOLY

ALIGNED

Places the dimension line parallel to a line drawn through the first and second insertion points.

Syntax

```
DIM: ALIGNED
First extension line origin or RETURN
    to select:
Select line, arc, or circle:
Dimension line location:
Dimension text <measured length>:
```

Description

This is a dimensioning command that is available only from the Dim: prompt. See the descriptions for DIM and DIM1 for information about dimensioning.

ANGULAR

Measures the angle between two lines.

Syntax

```
DIM: ANGULAR
Select first line:
Second line:
Enter dimension line arc location:
Dimension text <measured angle>:
Enter text location:
```

Description

This is a dimensioning command that is available only from the Dim: prompt. See the descriptions for DIM and DIM1 for information about dimensioning.

If you press Return at the Enter text location: prompt, AutoCAD will place the text in the dimension arc. Otherwise, the text will be entered at the location you indicate. If the text does not fit, you will be prompted:

```
Text does not fit. Enter new text
    location:
```

APERTURE

Controls the size of the aperture box in OSNAP modes.

Syntax
```
Command: APERTURE
Object snap target height (1-50
    pixels) <current>:
```

Description
The size of the aperture can be changed to fit the way you want to work. If you make the size of the aperture too small, it will be difficult to determine whether entities pass through. If the aperture is too large, too many entities will pass through, and the wrong entity may be selected. You may have to try several settings to determine the best size.

ARC

Draws an arc segment.

Syntax
```
Command: ARC
Center/<Start point>:
Center/End/<Second point>:
End point:
```

Description

At each prompt, you enter a point. AutoCAD does not recognize a straight line as an arc of infinite radius. If the three points lie on a straight line, AutoCAD will display an error message.

There are several methods for entering points to define an arc. The Center option allows you to indicate the center for the arc. The <Start point> option indicates the starting point for the arc, and the End option indicates the end point for the arc. The <Second point> option indicates a point along the arc.

The Radius option allows you to enter a radius for the arc. The Direction option prompts you for the tangent direction of the arc, and the Angle option prompts you for the included angle for the arc. The Length of chord option indicates the length of the chord for the arc.

AREA

Calculates the area of an object.

Syntax

```
Command: AREA
<First point>/Entity/Add/Subtract:
```

Description

First point is the default. You can enter points clockwise or counterclockwise. You do not have to reenter the first point; AutoCAD automatically "closes" the area. Use the Entity option when you work with circles and polylines.

The Add option sets add mode and switches between adding and subtracting areas. The prompt changes to:

```
<First point>/Entity/Subtract:
```

As you add and subtract, AutoCAD keeps a running total of the area and displays this total as you work.

The Subtract option sets subtract mode.

ARRAY

Makes multiple copies of entities.

Syntax

Rectangular Arrays

```
Command: ARRAY
Select objects:
Rectangular or Polar array (R/P):R
Number of rows (—) <1>:
Number of columns (||||) <1>:
Unit cell or distance between rows
    (—):
Distance between columns (||||):
```

Description

Rectangular arrays are based on horizontal rows and vertical columns. *Unit cell* refers to vertical and horizontal distances between entities. If you indicate opposite corners of the array at the Unit cell prompt, AutoCAD skips the prompt for column distances.

To create a rotated array, use the Rotate option of the SNAP command, and rotate your snap grid.

Syntax

Polar Arrays

```
Command: ARRAY
Select objects:
Rectangular or Polar (R/P):P
Center point of array:
Number of items:
Angle to fill (+=CCW, -=CW) <360>:
```

```
Angle between items:
Rotate objects as they are copied?
    <Y>:
```

Description

Center point of array: is the point around which all entities are copied.

Number of items: is the number of copies you want.

Angle to fill: is the number of degrees you want these copies to fill.

Angle between items: is the angle that separates the entities in the array.

The last prompt asks whether the objects are to be rotated. AutoCAD will rotate the objects in accordance with the polar array.

You must provide information for at least two of these three prompts: Number of items:, Angle to fill:, and Angle between items:. If you do not want to give information at a prompt, press Return; the next prompt will appear.

ATTDEF

Creates an attribute definition that controls various aspects of textual information assigned to a block.

Syntax

```
Command: ATTDEF
Attribute modes — Invisible:N
    Constant:N Verify:N Preset:N
Enter (ICVP) to change, Return when
    done:
Attribute tag:
Attribute prompt:
```

```
Default Attribute value:
Start point or Align/Center/Fit/Middle
    /Right/Style:
Height <default>:
Rotation angle:
```

If you are working with Constant attributes, the following prompt will appear (instead of Default attribute value:):

```
    Attribute value:
```

Description

Attribute modes are settings that control various aspects of the attributes. There are four modes: Invisible, Constant, Verify, and Preset. These modes are set for each attribute you assign to a block, and may be different for each attribute in the block.

Invisible mode controls the visibility of the attributes when the block is inserted in the drawing.

Constant mode gives attributes a fixed (unchangeable) value.

Verify mode simply prompts you for the value you have entered for the attribute, so that you can verify the value.

Preset mode allows you to have variable attributes and not be prompted for the value upon insertion of the block.

Attribute tag: is the label for the attribute you are defining. All attributes associated with a single block must have different tags. Different blocks may have the same tags for their attributes.

Attribute prompt: depends on the setting for Constant mode. If the attribute is constant, there is no need for a prompt; the attributes will not change when the block is inserted. If the attributes are variable, the prompt is used when the blocks are inserted. You

create this prompt, which will appear at the command
area to indicate what information the attribute needs.
Spaces are accepted as spaces. Be sure to state clearly
the information in the prompt so that other operators
will understand and be able to use your library parts.

Attribute value: is the actual piece of information in the attribute. If your attributes are set constant,
this information will remain the same whenever you
insert this particular block.

The remaining prompts are the same as the TEXT
command prompts.

ATTDISP

Overrides the default visibility setting for all attributes.

Syntax

Command: ATTDISP
Normal/On/Off <current setting>:

Description

Normal defaults to the setting at which the attributes
were created.

On overrides the display settings and turns on all
attributes, making them visible. Off overrides the
display settings and turns off all attributes, making
them invisible.

ATTEDIT

Allows you to edit attributes.

Syntax

```
Command: ATTEDIT
Edit attributes one by one? <Y>:
Block name specification <*>:
Attribute tag specification <*>:
Attribute value specification <*>:
```

Description

At the `Edit attributes one by one? <Y>:` prompt, you tell AutoCAD whether you will edit one-by-one or globally. If you answer `Yes` (for one-by-one editing), you are restricted to the visible attributes. Prompts at each attribute allow you to change the location, angle, height, and other properties as well as the value. You can further limit the attributes edited by selecting certain block names, tags, or values for the attributes.

If you answer `No` (for global editing), you are not restricted to the visible attributes. You can specify the attributes you want to edit by indicating tag, value, or block name. When you edit globally, you can change only the value of the attribute.

After you have selected an editing mode, you need to specify block names, attribute tags, and attribute values. Use a comma to separate two or more names. You may use wild-card characters in the names—the asterisk (*) for many characters and the question mark (?) for a single character. Only the attributes you specify will be edited.

One-by-One Editing

If you are editing attributes one-by-one, the following prompt appears:

```
Select attributes:
```

The attributes are edited in reverse order (the last attribute selected is the first attribute you edit). This attribute is marked with an X, and the following prompt appears:

```
Value/Position/Height/Angle/Style/
    Layer/Color/Next<N>:
```

Value allows you to change the value set when you originally inserted the block, provided that the value is not Constant. AutoCAD prompts:

```
Change or Replace? <R>:
```

If you select Change, the following prompt appears:

```
String to change:
New string:
```

Type the string you need changed, press Return, and then type only the letters that need to be changed.

If you select Replace, AutoCAD prompts:

```
New attribute value:
```

Type the new value, and press Return.

Position allows you to specify a new location for the attribute.

Height allows you to change the height of the attribute text.

Angle allows you to change the angle of the text's base line.

Style refers to the text font or style used.

Layer allows you to change the layer on which the attribute resides.

Color allows you to change the color for the attributes.

When you finish with one attribute, AutoCAD moves the X to the next attribute to be edited. The same series of prompts is displayed for each attribute.

Global Editing

If you are editing attributes globally, AutoCAD displays the following set of prompts:

```
Global edit of Attribute values.
Edit only Attributes visible on
   screen? <Y>:
```

If you answer `Yes`, AutoCAD prompts you for any block names, tags, or values for restricting the editing of the attributes. The attributes are limited to those visible on the screen.

If you answer `No`, AutoCAD tells you that the drawing will be regenerated after the editing process and prompts you to select any block names, tags, or values for restriction of the editing process.

When you have set specifications, if any, for the block names, tags, and values, you will see the following prompt for editing visible attributes only:

```
Select Attributes:
```

AutoCAD indicates with an `X` the attribute currently being edited. You are prompted:

```
String to change:
New string:
```

These prompts will proceed until all the attributes indicated have been edited.

If you edit all the attributes, AutoCAD switches to text mode. You are prompted:

```
String to change:
New string:
```

AutoCAD searches the attributes you have selected. The first time it encounters the string to change, AutoCAD replaces that string and prompts you for a new string to change. If you press Return at the `String to change:` prompt, AutoCAD places the new string at the beginning of all the attributes. When you are finished editing, press Return at both prompts.

ATTEXT

Allows extraction of attribute information from a drawing.

Syntax

```
Command: ATTEXT
CDF, SDF, or DXF Attribute extract (or
    Entities)? <C>
Template file <default>:
Extract file name <drawing name>:
```

Description

Indicate the form you want the extracted file to take by using CDF, Comma Delimited Format; SDF, similar to dBASE III®'s SDF format; or DXF, AutoCAD's Drawing Interchange File format. Next you input a Template file to tell AutoCAD how to structure the data in the extract file. (See the *AutoCAD Reference Manual* for information on how to create a template file.)

Finally, you enter the Extract file name for the extracted information.

AXIS

Sets up an axis of tick marks on the bottom and right side of the drawing area.

Syntax

```
Command: AXIS
Tick spacing (x) or ON/OFF/Snap/Aspect
    <current>:
```

Description

Tick spacing is the default. Type a value at the prompt to set the spacing for both X and Y axes.

ON turns on the axis after the spacing is set; OFF turns off the axis.

Snap sets the axis to current snap value.

Aspect allows differing X and Y values for spacing.

BASE

Creates the insertion point when you want to insert one drawing into another.

Syntax

```
Command: BASE
Base point <current>:
```

Description

The default is 0,0,0 World Coordinate System.

BASELINE

Allows you to utilize the last dimension you input as a base point for the next dimension entered.

Syntax

```
DIM: BASELINE
Second extension line origin:
Dimension text <value>:
```

Description

This dimensioning command is available only from the Dim: prompt. See the descriptions for DIM and DIM1 for information about dimensioning.

Note that because AutoCAD uses the first extension line origin of the last dimension you input as the basc point, you are prompted for the Second extension line origin without being prompted for the first.

BLIPMODE

Toggles blips on and off.

Syntax

```
Command: BLIPMODE
ON/OFF <current>:
```

Description

Blips are the small + symbols that AutoCAD inserts whenever you input a point or select an entity.

BLOCK

Creates an object from existing entities.

Syntax

```
Command: BLOCK
Block name (or ?):
Insertion base point:
Select objects:
```

Description

Blocks are library parts created from objects existing in

AutoCAD. If you are using Release 10, the blocks will be truly three-dimensional; earlier releases have two-dimensional blocks only.

To list all the blocks you have created, enter a question mark (?), and press Return at the first prompt. A complete listing of the blocks currently in the drawing will scroll on-screen.

The Block name may be 31 characters long and contain letters, numbers, the dollar sign ($), the hyphen (-), and the underscore (_). AutoCAD automatically converts letters to uppercase. If the block exists, AutoCAD prompts:

```
Block _____ already exists.
Redefine it? <N>:
```

When you redefine a block, be sure not to redefine it to itself; that is, don't take an inserted block and redefine the block to its current name. To redefine a block, either redraw the entire block, or use the EXPLODE command.

Insertion base point: is the reference point AutoCAD uses to pull the library part back to the drawing. When you identify the insertion base point, you are prompted to select objects.

BREAK

Removes parts of an entity or separates an entity into segments.

Syntax

```
Command: BREAK
Select object:
Enter first point (or F for First):
Enter second point:
```

Description

With the last two prompts, AutoCAD is looking for the two points used to indicate the segment to be removed.

If the two points are on a line, the part of the line between the two points will be removed. If one point is beyond the end of the line, the end of the line will be removed.

Parts are removed from an arc in the same way that parts are removed from a line. Circles must be broken with the second point counterclockwise from the first.

A polyline is broken between the two points. If there is a nonzero width, the ends are cut square. If you have fit a curve to the polyline, the information becomes permanent. On the tablet menu, there are two BREAK commands: BREAK and BREAK @. BREAK removes parts of an entity. BREAK @ separates the entity without removing a part. If you are using BREAK @, you will be prompted for a first point. That first point is where the entity will be divided.

CENTER

Marks center of a circle or arc.

Syntax

```
DIM: CENTER
Select arc or circle:
```

Description

This dimensioning command is available only from the Dim: prompt. See the descriptions for DIM and DIM1 for information about dimensioning.

This subcommand places a cross (+) at the center of the entity you select.

CHAMFER

Trims or extends two lines until specified distances are met, and then connects the lines with a line segment.

Syntax

```
Command: CHAMFER
Polyline/Distances/<Select first
    line>:
Select second line:
Enter first chamfer distance
    <current>:
Enter second chamfer distance
    <current>:
```

Description

At the `Polyline/Distance/<Select first line>:` prompt, the distances default to 0. To set these distances to the correct value, type **D** at this prompt. The first distance is applied to the first line you will select; the second, to the second line you will select. After specifying the distances, repeat the CHAMFER command and select the lines.

If you type **P** at the `Polyline/Distance/ <Select first line>:` prompt, AutoCAD will allow you to chamfer polylines. AutoCAD will not chamfer parallel lines.

CHANGE

Modifies entities.

Syntax

```
Command: CHANGE
Select objects:
Properties/<Change point>:
```

Description

There are two ways to change entities: by indicating a `Change point` or by changing the `Properties`. A change point will modify the physical entity. Properties are color, linetype, layer, and a few other selections.

The effect of using a `Change point` on various entities is slightly different.

❏ **Line**. The end of the line closest to the change point will move to the change point. Several lines may be indicated.

❏ **Circle**. The radius is changed so that the circumference passes through the change point.

❏ **Text**. The location of the text is changed. The insertion point for the text is moved to the change point. If you press Return at the `Properties/<Change point>:` prompt, AutoCAD will prompt for a new text style, text height, rotation angle, and text string. You can change all aspects of text. There are some exceptions, however. If the text is defined with a fixed height you cannot change the height of that particular font.

❏ **Block**. You can provide a new insertion point by indicating a change point.

If you select `Properties`, AutoCAD displays the following prompt:

```
Change what property (Color/Elev/
    LAyer/LType/Thickness)? :
```

`Color` changes the color of an entity. If you have overridden the layer color and want the entity to default to the layer color, type **BYLAYER**. This tells AutoCAD to set colors by layer. You will be prompted with the following:

```
New color <current>:
```

If the current color is BYBLOCK, the entities are set to the color of the block in which they reside. You may also use this setting to override the layer color setting. Type the color, by number or by name, that you want the entity to have:

1	Red
2	Yellow
3	Green
4	Cyan
5	Blue
6	Magenta
7	White

Elev stands for elevation and will change the location of the entities with respect to the Z axis.

LAyer changes the layer on which an entity resides. If the destination layer is off, the entity will disappear from the screen when you are finished with the CHANGE command. If the entity's color and linetype are set BYLAYER, the entity will acquire the settings for the new layer.

LType changes the linetype of the entities. The comments listed under the LINETYPE command apply here. Again, if you change the linetype of an entity, you are overriding the layer setting unless you are changing the linetype to BYLAYER.

Thickness modifies the thickness of the entities.

CHPROP

Modifies properties of entities.

Syntax

```
Command: CHPROP
Select objects:
Change what property (Color/LAyer/
    LType/Thickness)?:
```

Description

This is a subset of the CHANGE command, changing only the properties of entities. See the description for the CHANGE command.

CIRCLE

Draws a circle.

Syntax

```
Command: CIRCLE
3P/2P/TTR/<Center point>:
```

Description

3P prompts you for three points. The circle is drawn with its circumference lying on the three points.

2P prompts you for two points. The two points define the circle's location and its diameter.

TTR is the Tangent/Tangent/Radius selection. The entities to which you want the circle to be tangent must be on-screen.

COLOR

Sets the color to draw entities with.

Syntax

```
Command: COLOR
New entity color <current>:
```

Description

You can respond to the prompt by typing the name (for standard colors) or the number of the color you want to draw with, by pressing Return to accept the current setting, or by typing **BYLAYER** or **BYBLOCK**.

BYLAYER causes the color of entities to default to the layer color setting. This means that the entities will be the color assigned to the layer on which they reside.

BYBLOCK causes the color of the entities to default to the color set for the block definition. The color of the block is determined when you create the block.

CONTINUE

Allows you to use the last dimension inserted as a reference for the next dimension. The second extension line of the first dimension is used as the first extension line for the new dimension.

Syntax

```
DIM: CONTINUE
Second extension line origin:
Dimension text <value>:
```

Description

This dimensioning command is available only from the Dim: prompt. See the descriptions for DIM and DIM1 for information about dimensioning.

CONTINUE is similar to BASELINE. The difference is that CONTINUE uses the second extension line origin of the last dimension as the first extension line origin of the current dimension. This keeps the dimension lines the same distance from the extension lines, when possible.

COPY

Copies selected objects.

Syntax

```
Command: COPY
Select objects:
<Base point or displacement>/Multiple:
```

Description

`Base point` provides AutoCAD a reference from which to act on these entities. `displacement` allows you to enter a displacement for X, Y, and Z coordinates. If you indicate a `Base point or displacement`, you will be prompted:

```
Second point of displacement:
```

With `Base point`, indicate the second point. With `displacement`, press Return.

`Multiple` allows you to make multiple copies at one time. If you indicate `Multiple`, you will be prompted:

```
Base point:
```

AutoCAD still needs a reference. With `Multiple`, you may want the base point to be on the object you are copying. This will make the copying easier to calculate. You are then prompted:

```
Second point of displacement:
Second point of displacement:
Second point of displacement:
```

AutoCAD allows you to place copies as many times as necessary. When you finish copying the object, press Return.

DBLIST

Lists information about all the entities in your drawing.

Syntax
```
Command: DBLIST
```

Description
DBLIST stands for DataBase LIST. The information scrolls on the screen. You can stop the listing with Ctrl-S; press any key to resume. Press Ctrl-C to cancel the listing and Ctrl-Q to echo to the printer.

DDATTE

Allows attribute editing by means of a dialogue box.

Syntax
```
Command: DDATTE
Select block:
```

Description
This command displays a dialogue box and allows you to change entity attributes in an interactive fashion on the screen.

'DDEMODES

Allows layer-setting changes by means of a dialogue box.

Syntax
```
Command: 'DDEMODES
```

Description

This command displays a dialogue box and allows you to change layers and some layer information in an interactive fashion on the screen.

'DDLMODES

Changes layer properties by means of a dialogue box.

Syntax

Command: 'DDLMODES

Description

This command is related to DDEMODES—it displays a dialogue box and allows you to change some layer properties in an interactive fashion on the screen. You can change colors and linetypes, and freeze layers or turn them on and off.

'DDRMODES

Sets drawing aids by means of a dialogue box.

Syntax

Command: 'DDRMODES

Description

This command displays a dialogue box and allows you to change some layer properties (such as snap, grid, axis, ortho, and blips) in an interactive fashion on the screen.

DDUCS

Controls User Coordinate System by means of a dialogue box.

Syntax
```
Command: DDUCS
```

Description
This command displays a dialogue box and allows you to define or set the current UCS in an interactive fashion on the screen.

DELAY

Delays execution of the next command.

Syntax
```
Command: DELAY
Delay time in milliseconds:
```

Description
DELAY is used in developing AutoCAD scripts. It allows you to specify, in milliseconds, the amount of time to delay before returning control to either the user or the next script command.

DIAMETER

Provides diameter dimensions.

Syntax

```
DIM: DIAMETER
Select arc or circle:
Dimension text <measured diameter>:
```

Description

This dimensioning command is available only from the `Dim:` prompt. See the descriptions for DIM and DIM1 for information about dimensioning.

The point at which you select the arc or circle determines where the dimension appears.

DIM or DIM1

Sets dimensioning mode.

Syntax

```
Command: DIM
```

or

```
Command: DIM1
```

Description

DIM1 allows you to enter only one dimension and then returns you to the `Command:` prompt. DIM, however, places you in dimensioning mode, so that you can execute several dimensioning commands. The dimensioning commands are as follows:

ALIGNED	HOMETEXT
ANGULAR	HORIZONTAL
BASELINE	LEADER
CENTER	NEWTEXT
CONTINUE	RADIUS
DIAMETER	REDRAW
EXIT	ROTATED

STATUS   UPDATE
STYLE   VERTICAL
UNDO

For information about each of these dimensioning commands, see the appropriate command description in this
book.

To return to the `Command:` prompt after using the
DIM command, type **EXIT** at the `Dim:` prompt or press
Ctrl-C.

DIST

Calculates the distance from one point to another.

Syntax

```
Command: DIST
First point:
Second point:
Distance = <calculated distance>
Angle in X-Y plane = <angle>
Angle from X-Y plane = <angle>
Delta X = <X change> Delta Y = <Y
    change> Delta Z = <Z change>
```

Description

This returns the angle in the X-Y plane; the angle from
the X-Y plane for a line drawn between the two points;
and the change in X, Y, and Z values for both points.

DIVIDE

Divides the entity into equal parts.

Syntax

```
Command: DIVIDE
Select object to divide:
<Number of segments>/Block:
```

Description

If you type the number of segments, point entities will be used. If you select `Block`, you will be prompted for the name of the block.

DONUT or DOUGHNUT

Inserts a solid filled ring in your drawing.

Syntax

```
Command: DONUT or DOUGHNUT
Inside diameter:
Outside diameter:
Center of doughnut:
Center of doughnut:
```

Description

`Inside diameter` is the inside diameter of the doughnut. For solid, filled circles, set `Inside diameter` to 0.

`Outside diameter` is the outside diameter for the doughnut.

`Center` allows you to enter as many doughnuts as you need with a single command. If you undo this command, all the doughnuts drawn with this command will be undone.

DRAGMODE

Modifies dragging.

Syntax

```
Command: DRAGMODE
ON/OFF/Auto <current>:
```

Description

The ON option permits dragging when appropriate. The OFF option disables all dragging. With the Auto option, all commands that support dragging will drag.

When you work with complex objects, it may be less time-consuming to turn DRAGMODE off until you have finished.

DTEXT

Draws text dynamically.

Syntax

```
Command: DTEXT
Start point or Align/Center/Fit
/Middle/Right/Style:
First text line point:
Second text line point:
Height <0.20>:
Text:
```

Description

The difference between the DTEXT and TEXT commands is that DTEXT echoes the text on-screen as you type and allows multiple lines of text to be created.

AutoCAD gives you the same prompts as the TEXT command, and all selections have the same meaning.

When you use the `Align`, `Center`, `Fit`, `Middle`, or `Right` options, you must finish typing your text and press Return before AutoCAD will adjust the text. (See the TEXT command.)

DVIEW

Defines parallel or perspective screens dynamically.

Syntax

```
Command: DVIEW
Select objects:
CAmera/TArget/Distance/POints/PAn/
    Zoom/TWist/CLip/Hide/Undo/<eXit>:
```

Description

CAmera pulls up the slider bars. You can change the angle from which you are looking, either by using the slider bars or by typing in the new angle. The camera is rotated around the target.

TArget allows you to change your target—what you are looking at. The target is rotated around the camera.

Distance changes the distance between the camera and the target. This option turns on the perspective view.

POints allows location of both camera and target using X, Y, and Z coordinates. The target point is specified first; the default target is located in the center of the viewport on the current UCS X-Y plane.

PAn is just like standard PAN, only dynamic.

Zoom allows you to adjust the camera's lens length if perspective is on. If perspective is off, you have a standard zoom center. The default camera length is approximately 50mm long—or what you would see through a "normal" lens on a 35mm camera.

TWist allows you to tilt or twist the view around the line of sight. (This command uses a camera-target setup to define the line of sight.)

CLip allows you to define clipping planes. This is how you define cutaways in your drawing. AutoCAD blanks whatever is in front of the front clipping plane or whatever is behind the back clipping plane. You receive the following prompt:

> Back/Front/<Off>:

Back blocks objects behind the back clipping plane. The following prompt appears:

> ON/OFF/distance from target
>   <current>:

Front blocks objects between you (the camera) and the front clipping plane. The following prompt appears:

> ON/OFF/Eye/distance from target
>   <current>:

If Eye is selected, the clipping plane is positioned at the camera.

<Off> turns off perspective view; use Distance to turn on perspective.

Hide removes hidden lines from the currently selected entities.

Undo will undo the last DVIEW option executed. If you use more than one option, you can step back through the whole command.

eXit ends the DVIEW command.

DXBIN

Loads compacted binary files, such as those produced by the AutoShade™ program.

Syntax

```
Command: DXBIN
DXB file:
```

Description

After executing DXBIN, enter the name of the binary file you want to load. For a more detailed description of this file, see the *AutoCAD Reference Manual*.

DXFIN

Loads drawing-interchange or normal binary files.

Syntax

```
Command: DXFIN
File name:
```

Description

Enter an empty or new drawing to load an entire DXF file to ensure that any layering, blocks, linetypes, text styles, and so on are generated correctly. If you are working in a drawing that already has these elements, only entity information should be loaded.

DXFOUT

Writes the current drawing file to a drawing interchange file or a binary file.

Syntax

```
Command: DXFOUT
File name <default>:
Enter decimal places of accuracy (0 to
    16)/Entities/Binary <6>:
```

Description

Enter the name of the file to contain the drawing information. The `Enter decimal places of accuracy` prompt defines the accuracy of the stored information. You can indicate specific `Entities` to be written, or you can specify a `Binary` file.

EDGESURF

Constructs a `Coons surface patch`—a polygon mesh bounded on four sides by entities you select.

Syntax

```
Command: EDGESURF
Select edge 1:
Select edge 2:
Select edge 3:
Select edge 4:
```

Description

Edges may be lines, arcs, or open polylines and must connect end to end. The M direction is determined by the first entity you indicate; the N direction is determined by the two entities connected to the first. The system variable SURFTAB1 controls divisions along the M direction, and the system variable SURFTAB2 controls divisions in the other directions.

ELEV

Controls where the current X-Y construction plane is located on the Z axis.

Syntax

```
Command: ELEV
New current elevation <current>:
New current thickness <current>:
```

Description

The X-Y plane can be moved up and down the Z axis
(elevation), and subsequently drawn entities can extrude
above or below the construction plane (thickness).

ELLIPSE

Draws ellipses.

Syntax

```
Command: ELLIPSE
<Axis endpoint 1>/Center:
Axis endpoint 2:
<Other axis distance>/Rotation:
```

or

```
Command: ELLIPSE
<Axis endpoint 1>/Center: C
Center of ellipse:
Axis endpoint:
<Other axis distance>/Rotation:
```

Description

The first set of prompts are the default prompts. Use
the second set of prompts for the Center selection.

To draw ellipses, AutoCAD uses both their major and
minor axes. AutoCAD uses the axis distances to set up
the ellipse. The default prompts ask you to indicate one
axis and then the endpoint for the other axis. After you
indicate the first axis, you are prompted for the endpoint of the second axis. AutoCAD is looking for a

distance to apply to the second axis. If the distance is shorter than half of the first axis, the first axis is the major axis. If the distance is longer, the first axis is the minor axis.

The second way to draw ellipses involves entering the center point for the ellipse. You then are prompted for a point to define one of the axes. The next prompt asks for the endpoint of the second axis. The last prompt line has another selection— Rotation. Using the first axis as the major axis, AutoCAD rotates the ellipse around that axis.

END

Saves your drawing and returns you to the Main Menu.

Syntax

```
Command: END
```

Description

Similar in purpose to the QUIT command, this is the way to end a drawing and return to the main AutoCAD menu.

ERASE

Removes entities from your drawing.

Syntax

```
Command: ERASE
Select objects:
Select objects:
```

Description

Select the objects you want to erase and then, at the
second prompt, press Return to execute the command.

EXIT

Returns you to the `Command:` prompt.

Syntax

```
DIM: EXIT
```

Description

This dimensioning command is available only from the
`Dim:` prompt. See the descriptions for DIM and DIM1
for information about dimensioning.

This command is used to leave the dimensioning mode
and return to the AutoCAD `Command:` prompt. You
may also press Ctrl-C to effect a similar result.

EXPLODE

Separates a block into its original entities.

Syntax

```
Command: EXPLODE
Select block reference, polyline,
    dimension or mesh:
```

Description

Select the block you want to break apart. The block
will "blink" on the screen. Special color or layer
assignments no longer exist. All entities are moved to
layer 0 and become white.

When you need to modify a block, you must explode the block, modify it, and then redefine the block.

EXTEND

Extends entities to a boundary.

Syntax

```
Command: EXTEND
Select boundary edge(s)...
Select objects:
```

Description

The entity or entities to be extended must be visible on the screen, and there must be a boundary. The first two prompts are looking for the boundaries to which you will extend. When all boundaries have been selected, press Return. You will then be prompted to select the object to extend.

FILES

Allows you to do some limited system operations while still in AutoCAD.

Syntax

```
Command: FILES
```

Description

You are able to list, delete, rename, and copy files. This is a menu-driven operation.

FILL

Controls the solid fill of polylines and solids.

Syntax

```
Command: FILL
ON/OFF <current>:
```

Description

If FILL is ON, the objects will be filled with color; if FILL is OFF, the outlines of the entities will appear on the screen.

FILLET

Trims or extends two entities and places a fillet between them.

Syntax

```
Command: FILLET
Polyline/Radius/<Select two objects>:
```

Description

When you select Polyline, AutoCAD prompts for the polyline to fillet. All segments that are long enough will be filleted.

The default Radius is 0; filleting entities with this radius causes the entities to be trimmed or extended to a sharp corner. To change the radius, type **R** at the prompt. AutoCAD prompts for the new radius:

```
Enter fillet radius <current>:
```

After you enter the radius, AutoCAD will end the FILLET command and return you to the Command: prompt. The radius you entered will remain until you change it.

FILMROLL

Generates a file used for rendering if you are using AutoShade.

Syntax

```
Command: FILMROLL
Enter the filmroll file name
    <default>:
```

Description

If you do not enter a specific file name, the current drawing is used as the default.

'GRAPHSCR

Switches a single-screen system from text display to graphics display.

Syntax

```
Command: 'GRAPHSCR
```

Description

The opposite of the TEXTSCR command, this command switches from a text to the graphics (drawing editor) screen. You also can use the F1 key to do the same task.

GRID

Sets up a rectangular array of reference points within the drawing limits.

Syntax

```
Command: GRID
Grid spacing (x) or ON/OFF/Snap/
  Aspect<current>:
```

Description

Grid spacing is the default and sets both the X and the Y value for the grid. When you enter a value and press Return, the grid automatically turns on at your setting.

When the grid is set up, you can toggle it on and off. The ON option toggles the grid on; the OFF option toggles the grid off.

By default, the grid setting is equal to the snap setting. If you want your grid to default to the snap setting, use the Snap option.

Aspect is used to set differing X and Y values for the grid. You are prompted separately for the X value and then for the Y value. Remember to respond to both prompts.

Because the points on grids are not drawing entities, you cannot reference them physically.

When you are working with the grid on, you may receive a Grid is too dense error message. This message means that, because the grid points are too close together to show on the screen, AutoCAD will not place the grid. If this happens, and you need your grid, reset the grid to a larger value.

HANDLES

Controls the system variable for unique identifiers for entities.

Syntax

```
Command: HANDLES
ON/DESTROY:
```

Description

ON is the default. All entities have a handle defined.

DESTROY will destroy all entity handles in the drawing. Because this option is potentially dangerous, AutoCAD displays a special message. To destroy the handles, you must enter a special phrase.

HATCH

Performs hatching.

Syntax

```
Command: HATCH
Pattern (? or name/U,style) <default>:
Scale for pattern <default>:
Angle for pattern <default>:
Select objects:
```

Description

? provides a listing of the hatch patterns available with AutoCAD.

name,style. When you want to change the hatching style, type the name of the pattern followed by a comma and the first letter of the style type: **N** for normal, **O** for outermost, or **I** for ignore. The default style is normal.

U,style allows you to describe your own pattern. You are prompted for the angle for the lines, the spacing between the lines, and whether you want the area double-hatched:

```
Angle for crosshatch lines
    <default>:
Spacing between lines <default>:
Double hatch area? <default>:
```

Scale. If you are working with a large or small
drawing, you will want to change the scale of the hatch
pattern. You may have to experiment to determine what
scale is best.

Angle. All hatch patterns are created in reference to
the X axis. If you want to hatch a rotated object, and
you want the pattern to align with the object, enter the
rotation angle here.

'HELP or '?

Provides on-line documentation.

Syntax

```
Command: HELP or ?
Command name (Return for list):
```

Description

If you enter a command, you will receive the documentation for it. If you press Return, you will receive a
listing of all commands in AutoCAD, as well as some
general information. To use HELP within a command,
the apostrophe ('HELP or '?) is required.

When you first enter the Drawing Editor, the HELP
command is activated whenever you press Return
without typing anything else.

HIDE

Removes hidden lines.

Description

Based on database information, AutoCAD determines
which lines in your drawing would be hidden (behind
other entities) and then redraws the screen with those
lines removed. Using this command may take some time
if your drawing is large.

HOMETEXT

Returns dimension text to its home position.

Syntax

    DIM: HOMETEXT
    Select objects:

Description

This dimensioning command is available only from the
Dim: prompt. See the descriptions for DIM and DIM1
for information about dimensioning.

Dimension text has a default location. This is its "home"
position.

HORIZONTAL

Gives the horizontal (X) distance between two points.

Syntax

    DIM: HORIZONTAL
    First extension line origin or Return
        to select:

```
Second extension line origin:
Dimension line location:
Dimension text <value>:
```

Description

This dimensioning command is available only from the
Dim: prompt. See the descriptions for DIM and DIM1
for information about dimensioning.

ID

Returns the coordinates of a point.

Syntax

```
Command: ID
Point:
```

Description

There does not have to be an entity at the point. You
can use OSNAP modes to snap onto parts of entities to
define specific points.

IGESIN

Converts and loads files in Initial Graphics Exchange
Standard (IGES).

Syntax

```
Command: IGESIN
File name:
```

Description

The use of IGES and related commands is beyond the
scope of this quick reference.

IGESOUT

Converts the current drawing to Initial Graphics Exchange Standard (IGES) format.

Syntax

```
Command: IGESOUT
File name:
```

Description

The use of IGES and related commands is beyond the scope of this quick reference.

INSERT

Inserts a previously defined block.

Syntax

```
Command: INSERT
Block name (or ?):
Insertion point:
X scale factor <1>/Corner/XYZ:
Y scale factor <default=X):
Rotation angle <0>:
```

Description

At the Block name (or ?): prompt, type the name of the block you want to insert.

Insertion point: prompts you for the location of the block. This is the point that will be aligned with the insertion base point you defined when you created the block.

At the X scale factor <1>/Corner/XYZ: prompt, you may enter a number or a point; or you can press Return if you want the block inserted at the scale drawn. If you enter a point, you can "show" AutoCAD the X and Y scales at the same time. The default value for the scale factor is 1; this value causes the block to be inserted at the scale at which it was drawn. (The XYZ option is available only with the ADE-3 package.)

At the Y scale factor <default=X): prompt, you can enter a differing Y scale factor from the X. If you want the X scale factor to be the same as the Y scale factor, press Return.

Negative scale values are acceptable. A negative X value "mirrors" the block around the Y axis; a negative Y value "mirrors" the block around the X axis.

With the Rotation angle <0>: prompt, the block is rotated around the insertion point at the given angle. If you accept the default angle of 0, the block is inserted at the orientation created. Angle input is applied counterclockwise.

ISOPLANE

Changes the orientation of the crosshairs when you are working in isometrics.

Syntax
```
Command: ISOPLANE
Left/Top/Right/(Toggle):
```

Description
The ISOPLANE command is a toggle; to change between the different settings, simply press Return at the prompt.

LAYER

Creates and modifies layers.

Syntax

```
Command: LAYER
?/Make/Set/New/ON/OFF/Color/Ltype/
    Freeze/Thaw:
```

Description

? gives you a listing of layers and their status.

Make is a combination of Set and New. When you use Make, you are prompted for the layer you want to be the current layer. AutoCAD searches for the layer name. If it is not found, AutoCAD creates a new layer with that name and sets that layer.

Set tells AutoCAD which layer you want to draw on.

The New option creates new layers. You are prompted for the layer names. To enter more than one layer name at a time, type the name followed by a comma and the next name; no spaces are allowed. Do not end your list with a comma.

ON turns on layers. When you create a new layer, it defaults to on. OFF turns off layers. When layers are off, you cannot see the entities, if any, that exist on those layers.

The Color option allows you to set the layer color. AutoCAD is capable of producing 255 colors. You will be limited, however, if your graphics card and monitor are not capable of producing that many colors. The following colors are standard:

1	Red	5	Blue
2	Yellow	6	Magenta
3	Green	7	White
4	Cyan		

The default color for new layers is white. Setting the
color also defines the color of the entities that reside on
a given layer.

Ltype sets the linetype for the layer. The default is the
solid linetype.

Freeze. Freezing layers is a time-saver. When you
freeze a layer, AutoCAD ignores the entities on that
layer. When a regeneration is executed, the time factor
is reduced.

Thaw allows you to access frozen layers. AutoCAD
automatically turns on thawed layers.

LEADER

Allows you to place notes in a drawing.

Syntax

```
DIM: LEADER
Leader start point:
To point:
To point:
Dimension text <last dimension
    entered>:
```

Description

This dimensioning command is available only from the
Dim: prompt. See the descriptions for DIM and DIM1
for information about dimensioning.

When you finish entering end points, press Return. You
will be prompted for the text you want inserted. The
default text is the last dimension entered in AutoCAD.

Respond to the To point: prompts as you would for
a normal LINE command. You can undo LEADER
segments if you want.

LIMITS

Controls drawing size.

Syntax

```
Command: LIMITS
ON/Off/<LLC> <current value>:
Upper right corner <12.00,9.00>:
```

Description

ON engages the limits check—a beep which warns you that you are outside the limits. OFF turns off the limits check.

LLC is the lower left corner of your drawing area. The default (0,0) is the standard setting for LIMITS. You may either press Return to accept 0,0 as the lower left corner, or you may enter a point by either digitizing or typing the X and Y values.

Upper right corner <12.00,9.00>: is where you set up the upper right corner of your drawing. Remember that the X (horizontal) value comes first, followed by the Y (vertical) value.

To see the new drawing size, type **ZOOM**, press Return, type **A**, and press Return again; your new drawing size will appear on-screen.

LINE

Draws a straight line.

Syntax

```
Command: LINE
From point:
To point:
To point:
```

Description

From point: prompts you for the beginning of the first line segment. You may enter this point by using any of the methods available for entering points.

To point: You are being prompted for the end of the current line segment. The point you enter at this prompt is used as the beginning for the next line segment. If you press Return without entering a point, you will end the LINE command.

You may type **U** at the To point: prompt. This will undo the last line segment you drew. If you remain in the LINE command while you undo the segment, AutoCAD allows you to pick up the line segments at the previous point entered.

If you type **C** at the prompt, AutoCAD will automatically close the sequence of lines. You must have two or more line segments to close the LINE command.

LINETYPE

Creates, loads, and sets linetypes.

Syntax

Command: LINETYPE
?/Create/Load/Set:

Description

? lists the linetypes available in a linetype file. You will be prompted:

File to list <acad>:

You will be returned to the LINETYPE prompt.

Create enables you to create primitive linetypes.

If a linetype is in a file other than ACAD.LIN, you must use the `Load` option to load it. You will be prompted:

```
Name of linetype to load:
File to search <default>:
```

The `Set` option sets the linetype with which you will be working. All the entities you draw from this point will be drawn in the linetype you set. If you draw a block with some entities set to layer default linetypes (some with linetype overrides, and some set to linetype by block), there will be confusion when the block is inserted. Some entities will retain the linetype you want, and other entities will change to the layer default. You are prompted:

```
New entity linetype <current>:
```

As with all overrides, be careful about changing the entities in your drawing. Use the overrides with caution.

The linetype for entities may be overridden in the same fashion as the colors.

LIST

Lists information for entities in your drawing.

Syntax

```
Command: LIST
Select objects:
```

Description

To echo the information to your printer, use Ctrl-Q before the command is executed.

LOAD

Loads compiled shape and font files.

Syntax

```
Command: LOAD
Name of shape file to load (or ?):
```

Description

Only shape files that have been successfully compiled
at the Main Menu can be loaded.

LTSCALE

Changes the scale of linetypes in your drawing.

Syntax

```
Command: LTSCALE
New scale factor <default>:
```

Description

Enter a value greater than 0 for the scale; the default
for new drawings is 1. You may have to set the scale a
few times to get the correct spacing on your linetypes.
You must execute the REGEN command after you set
LTSCALE. Type **REGEN** at the Command: prompt,
and press Return.

MEASURE

Measures a distance, placing points or markers at
intervals.

```
Command: MEASURE
Select object to measure:
<Segment length>/Block:
```

Description

Select the object with which you will work. Type the
length or **B** for Block. The lengths will be measured
from the end of the entity nearest the point at which
you selected that entity. If you are using the Block
option, you will be prompted for the name of the block.
MEASURE can use only a block that has been created
and is already in the drawing.

MENU

Allows you to work with menus other than the standard
AutoCAD menu.

Syntax
```
Command: MENU
Menu file name or . for none
    <current>:
```

Description

Enter the name of the new menu you want to work
with. AutoCAD supports screen, button, tablet, and
pull-down menus.

MINSERT

Makes multiple inserts of a block.

Syntax

```
Command: MINSERT
Block name (or ?):
Insertion point:
X scale factor <1>/Corner/XYZ:
Y scale factor <default = X>:
Rotation angle <0>:
```

Description

These are the standard INSERT prompts; see the
INSERT command for an explanation of the options.
The only difference is that you cannot enter a block
name with an asterisk (*) to insert the block exploded.
Following are the prompts for the array part of the
MINSERT command:

```
Number of rows (—) <1>:
Number of columns (| | |) <1>:
```

Type the number of rows and the number of columns.
If the number of rows is greater than 1, you will be
prompted for the distance between the rows or for a
unit cell:

```
Unit cell or distance between rows
   (—)
```

A unit cell includes both the block and the distance
between the rows. AutoCAD needs to know the
distance from one entity in the first block to the same
entity in the second block.

MIRROR

Reflects entities on an axis.

Syntax

```
Command: MIRROR
Select objects:
```

```
First point of mirror line:
Second point:
Delete old objects? <N>:
```

Description

Select the objects with which you want to work. Because the `mirror line` is a line of symmetry in the final object, its placement is important. At the next two prompts, specify the first and second points that will define this line.

You can retain the original entities or delete them with the `Delete old objects? <N>:` prompt.

MOVE

Moves entities in the drawing.

Syntax

```
Command: MOVE
Select objects:
Base point or displacement:
Second point of displacement:
```

Description

`Base point` gives AutoCAD a reference for moving the entities. This is equivalent to the insertion base point for blocks.

`displacement`. AutoCAD will accept a displacement for the entities. You must enter at least an X and Y value; AutoCAD will accept X, Y, and Z values. The displacement should correspond to the X, Y, and Z displacements for the entities.

`Second point`. No matter how you respond to the previous prompt, you will be prompted for a second point. If you entered a `displacement`, press Return at this prompt. If you indicated a `Base point`, either "show" AutoCAD where you want the entities by dragging them, or indicate the coordinates for the second point.

MSLIDE

Makes a slide of a drawing or part of a drawing.

Syntax

```
Command: MSLIDE
Slide file <default>:
```

Description

Before you execute the MSLIDE command, pull up the drawing in the Drawing Editor, and zoom in on the area that you want to be the slide.

AutoCAD needs to know the name of the slide file. The name must be a DOS file name—up to eight characters, with the standard DOS limitations. AutoCAD creates the slide from what is displayed on-screen.

MULTIPLE

Repeats another command until canceled.

Syntax

```
Command: MULTIPLE
```

Description

This command is used in concert with another command and will keep repeating the other command until Ctrl-C is executed. For example, if you are inserting several blocks and will be using the INSERT command

often, type **MULTIPLE INSERT** at the `Command:`
prompt; INSERT will keep repeating until you cancel.

NEWTEXT

Allows you to change the text in an existing dimension.

Syntax

```
DIM: NEWTEXT
Enter new dimension text:
Select objects:
```

Description

This dimensioning command is available only from the
`Dim:` prompt. See the descriptions for DIM and DIM1
for information about dimensioning.

OFFSET

Creates a parallel entity next to the original.

Syntax

```
Command: OFFSET
Offset distance or Through <last>:
```

Description

If you type an `Offset distance`, all offsets will be
that distance. The following set of prompts appears:

```
Select object to offset:
Side to offset:
```

You select the entity to offset and then specify a point
on the side of that entity on which you want to place
the offset.

If you selected `Through`, you will be prompted for the point through which the new entity will pass. The following prompts appear for each entity:

```
Select object to offset:
Through point:
```

AutoCAD is looking for the entity to offset and the point through which the new entity will pass. One problem arises in OFFSET when you try to offset complex curves such as ellipses and other polylines and arc generations. If you offset to the interior of the curve, AutoCAD, reaching a point at which it is not sure how to draw the next curve, will improvise.

OOPS

Brings back the last group of entities erased.

Syntax
```
Command: OOPS
```

Description
Similar in purpose to the UNDO or U commands, this is a way to undo or negate your previous edits.

ORTHO

Restricts user to horizontal or vertical movement of the cursor.

Syntax
```
Command: ORTHO
ON/OFF:
```

Description

Pressing Return at the prompt toggles ORTHO on or off.

= OSNAP

Sets global Object SNAP modes.

Syntax

```
Command: OSNAP
Object snap modes:
```

Description

OSNAP modes can be used globally, as with the OSNAP command, or individually. If the mode is set globally, the mode will be invoked whenever AutoCAD looks for point information. To use the modes selectively, type in the appropriate mode at the prompt for point information, and press Return. You will be prompted for the entity with which you want to work.

You may indicate modes by typing just the first three letters of the mode name.

NEArest locates a point visually nearest the crosshairs on the entity and snaps to that point.

ENDpoint is the closest endpoint of a line or arc, or the closest defining point of a solid or three-dimensional face. You can snap to the extruded points of these entities.

MIDpoint snaps to the midpoint of lines, arcs, polyline segments, and the extruded sides of entities, and can be applied to solids and three-dimensional faces by snapping to the midpoint between the two nearest corners.

CENter snaps to the center of arcs and circles. When using this OSNAP mode, you must indicate the entity by digitizing the circumference. AutoCAD locates the center; you just need to indicate the entity with which you want to work.

NODe locks onto a point entity.

QUAdrant locks onto the closest point on a circle or arc at 0, 90, 180, or 270 degrees. You can use this mode only with entities that are in the current UCS or whose extrusion direction is parallel to the Z axis of the current UCS.

INTersection locks onto an intersection only if it is a true intersection in three-dimensional space. For extruded entities, you can lock onto the intersection of the entity and the extrusion lines. If two entities intersect on a UCS and extrude in the same direction, AutoCAD can locate the intersection of the extruded edges. If there is a difference in the amount of extrusion, the shorter extrusion defines the intersection. Make sure that both entities are in the aperture when you indicate the intersection.

INSert locks onto the insertion points of blocks, text, and shapes.

PERpendicular locks onto an existing entity in such a way that the new entity is perpendicular to the last point entered on the existing entity. Any extrusion must be parallel to the current UCS Z axis. This mode is used in reference to the last point entered.

TANgent locks onto a point on an entity that is tangent to the last point entered. Any extrusion must be parallel to the current UCS Z axis.

NONe cancels any globally set OSNAP modes. Simply type **NONE** at the Object snap modes: prompt, and press Return.

'PAN

Allows you to move around in the drawing without changing the zoom factor.

Syntax

```
Command: PAN
Displacement:
Second point:
```

Description

PAN needs two points. The first is a reference point; the second point indicates the direction and distance you want to pan.

At the Displacement: prompt, you can either type a displacement in x,y,z fashion, or you can indicate a point. If you type a displacement, press Return. If you indicate a point, type another point at the Second point: prompt to show direction and displacement.

PEDIT—2-D, 3-D

Allows you to edit polylines or meshes.

Syntax

```
Command: PEDIT
Select polyline:
```

If the entity you indicate is not a polyline, AutoCAD prompts:

```
Entity selected is not a polyline.
Do you want it to turn into one?
   <Y>:
```

A **Y** response turns the entity into a polyline. You will see the following prompt:

```
Close/Join/Width/Edit vertex/Fit
    curve/Spline curve/Decurve/Undo/
    eXit <X>:
```

Description

If the polyline selected is not closed, you can close it with the `Close` option. If the polyline is closed, the `Close` option becomes the `Open` option, and you have the option of opening the polyline.

`Join` attaches separate line and arc segments to one another, forming a polyline.

`Width` sets a uniform width for the entire polyline.

When you select the `Fit curve` option, AutoCAD fits a curve to the polyline. The curves are drawn to tangent points and pass through the vertices.

A `Spline curve` is different from a `Fit curve`. A spline is a best-fit curve to the polyline. This selection uses the vertices of the polyline as a frame to draw the spline. The more vertices there are, the more the curve will be "pulled" in that particular direction.

`Decurve` removes the fit curve or the spline from the polyline.

`Undo` will undo the last PEDIT operation you performed. You can use it to step back to the beginning of the PEDIT editing session.

To keep any changes you have made, you must use the `eXit` option to exit the PEDIT command.

`Edit vertex` allows you to edit individual segments by using the vertices. When you enter this selection, an X appears at the start of the polyline. The X indicates which segment you will be working with. When you select `Edit vertex`, AutoCAD displays the following prompt:

```
Next/Previous/Break/Insert/Move/
    Regen/Straighten/Tangent/Width/
    eXit <N>:
```

Next moves the indicator to the next vertex.

Previous moves the indicator to the previous vertex.

Break removes a segment of the polyline or breaks the polyline into separate entities. You will see a new prompt:

Next/Previous/Go/eXit <N>:

Next and Previous move the indicator. The command will be executed for the segments you cross while at this prompt. Go executes the selection, and eXit leaves the selection without executing.

Insert inserts a new vertex between the current vertex and the next vertex. Move the cursor to the vertex directly before the new vertex, and then select Insert.

Move moves the current vertex to the specified new location.

Regen acts like the normal REGEN. After you change a segment's width, you must use Regen in order to see your changes.

Straighten removes all vertices between two indicated vertices. You are prompted:

Next/Previous/Go/eXit <N>:

Tangent provides the polyline tangent information used in Fit curve. You can define the angle to which you want the fitted curves to be tangent. Simply move to the vertex and enter the tangent angle. An indicator will appear on your screen.

Width allows you to change the width of individual segments. You must do a REGEN to see the change in the width. You will be prompted for both a new beginning width and a new ending width.

eXit returns you to the basic PEDIT prompt.

After you change the polyline, you can use the other editing commands. You can COPY, MOVE, ERASE,

ARRAY, MIRROR, ROTATE, and SCALE the
polyline. If these commands are executed, the Spline
will retain its frame. But if you BREAK, TRIM, or
EXPLODE the polyline, the frame will be deleted.
OFFSET creates a polyline fit to the Spline.

PEDIT (MESHES)

Allows you to edit polylines or meshes.

Syntax
    Command: PEDIT

Description

The following lists show how the PEDIT command
options react with a three-dimensional polygon mesh:

Decurve	Restores the original mesh.
Edit vertex	Edits the mesh vertexes individually.
M	Opens or closes the mesh in the M direction.
N	Opens or closes the mesh in the N direction.
S	Fits a smooth surface, using the SURFTYPE system variable.

These are the options for vertex editing:

D	Moves *down* in the M direction to the previous vertex.
L	Moves *left* in the N direction to the previous vertex.
M	Moves the indicated vertex.
R	Moves *right* in the N direction to the next vertex.
RE	Redisplays the mesh.
U	Moves *up* in the M direction to the next vertex.

PLAN

Provides a plan view of the drawing relative to the current UCS, a specified UCS, or the World Coordinate System.

Syntax

```
Command: PLAN
<Current UCS>/UCS/World:
```

Description

The <Current UCS> option provides the plan view with respect to the current User Coordinate System (UCS). With the UCS option, you are prompted for the name of the previously saved UCS for which you want a plan view. You can enter a question mark (?) for a listing of the currently defined UCSs.

World regenerates the drawing to a plan view of the World Coordinates.

PLINE

Draws polylines.

Syntax

```
Command: PLINE
From point:
Current line width is ___
Arc/Close/Halfwidth/Length/Undo/Width/
    <Endpoint of line>:
```

Description

The PLINE command needs a starting point for the segments. Indicate a starting point at the From point: prompt.

The default drawing segment is a line. You may indicate the `<Endpoint of line>:`, or select one of the other options.

The `Arc` option provides a different prompt:

```
Angle/CEnter/CLose/Direction/
    Halfwidth/Line/Radius/Second pt/
    Undo/Width/<Endpoint of arc>:
```

You can now draw arc segments in any of several ways. You can use the `Angle`, `CEnter`, `Direction`, `Radius`, and `Second pt` options as you would for the ARC command.

`Close` closes the current polyline.

`Halfwidth` allows you to specify half the width of a wide polyline. You are prompted:

```
Starting half-width <current>:
Ending half-width <current>:
```

`Length` allows you to enter the length of the segment. The segment is drawn at the same angle as the last segment.

`Undo` is used to undo the last part of the PLINE command. Undo in PLINE reacts the same as Undo in the LINE command.

`Width` allows you to assign widths to polyline segments.

`Endpoint` is the default. AutoCAD is looking for the end of the line segment.

PLOT

Plots a drawing on a pen plotter.

Syntax

```
Command: PLOT
What to plot — Display, Extents,
    Limits, View, or Window <D>:
```

Description

Display plots the current display—that part of the drawing displayed on-screen when the command is executed.

Extents plots the extents of the drawing. Before you plot extents, it is a good idea to ZOOM extents. If any entities lie beyond the drawing limits, they also are included in the extents.

Limits selects the limits you set up for your drawing. If you are using a title block, use this selection.

View plots a defined view. Use this for preliminary drawings in large projects.

Window plots an area that you "window." You are prompted for the two corners of the window.

After you specify what you want plotted, you are prompted:

```
Plot will NOT be written to a
    selected file.
Sizes are in inches
Plot origin is at (0.00,0.00)
Plotting area is xx wide by yy high
Plot is NOT rotated 90 degrees
Pen width is 0.010
Area fill will be adjusted for pen
    width
Hidden lines will NOT be removed
Plot will be scaled to fit available
    area
Do you want to change anything? <N>
```

These values are set up when you configure AutoCAD. If you accept the values, press Return at the prompt. If

you do not accept them, type **Y** and press Return.
AutoCAD will prompt for changes to the preceding
values.

The `Do you want to change anything?`
`<N>` prompt is where you set the speed of your plotting,
pen numbers for layers, and linetypes (see the following table for the default values). The pen numbers are
related to the colors of the entities. If you want to
change any of the settings for the pens, type **Y** at the
prompt. You are prompted for the pen number, linetype, and pen speed for entity color 1. You can respond
to these prompts in five ways. You can change the
value, press Return to retain the current value, type **C**n
where n is the pen number you want to jump to, type **S**
to show the updated table, or type **X** to resume the
PLOT prompts.

Entity Color	Pen No.	Line-type	Pen Speed
1 (red)	1	0	38
2 (yellow)	2	0	38
3 (green)	3	0	38
4 (cyan)	4	0	38
5 (blue)	5	0	38
6 (magenta)	6	0	38
7 (white)	7	0	38
8	8	0	38
9	1	0	38
10	1	0	38
11	1	0	38
12	1	0	38
13	1	0	38
14	1	0	38
15	1	0	38
16	1	0	38

After you have entered the changes for the pens, you
are prompted for basic plotting specifications.

With the `Write the plot to a file?` `<cur-`
`rent>` prompt, you can send plots to a file instead of

to the plotter. This can save time while you are working; the plotting can be done later.

You can work in inches or millimeters. The `Size units (Inches or Millimeters) <current>` prompt allows you to change the size units.

Regarding the `Plot origin in units <default X,Y>:` prompt, with pen plotters the origin is usually the lower left corner of the paper. This is the *home* position for the pen. For printer plotters, home is the upper left corner. The plot origin corresponds to the lower left corner of the drawing. AutoCAD allows you to move the plot origin. If you are working with D-size paper, you can plot four A-size drawings on the same paper by moving the plot origin.

With the `Enter the Size or Width,Height (in units) <default>:` prompt, AutoCAD allows entry of the plotting area you want to work with. The maximum size for plotting depends on the physical size of your plotter. Plotting size is measured from the plot origin; you can create a margin around the drawing by setting a new plot origin.

The `Rotate 2D plots 90 degrees clockwise? <N>` prompt allows you to rotate the plot 90 degrees. This means that the point which would have been in the lower left corner will now be in the upper left corner, and that all other corners will rotate accordingly.

If you are using wide polylines and solids, you may want to adjust the pen width with the `Pen width <default>` prompt. This affects the amount of work necessary to fill in these areas.

The `Adjust area fill boundaries for pen width? <N>` prompt adjusts the plotting of wide polylines and solids by half a pen width. This adjustment provides a more accurate plot. If you are plotting printed circuit artwork, for example, you will want to change the setting by typing **Y**. If you do not need the additional accuracy, you should respond **N**.

When you are plotting three-dimensional objects, you can remove the hidden lines by entering **Y** at the `Remove hidden lines? <N>` prompt. (You cannot do this for two-dimensional plots.)

With the `Specify scale by entering:` prompt, you can set the scale for the plot. This scale is independent of the drawing scale. You can scale either the drawing or the plot. You are prompted:

```
Specify scale by entering:
Plotted Inches=Drawing units or Fit
    or ? <F>:
```

If you are working with millimeters, the preceding prompt will say `Plotted Millimeters` instead of `Plotted Inches`.

POINT

Inserts point entities into your drawing.

Syntax

```
Command: POINT
Point:
```

Description

Point locations may be indicated in any fashion. You may use OSNAP modes, absolute coordinates, or relative coordinates.

POLYGON

Draws polygons.

Syntax

```
Command: POLYGON
Number of sides:
Edge/<Center of polygon>:
```

Description

When you enter the `<Center of polygon>:`, you are prompted:

```
Inscribed in circle/Circumscribed
    about circle (I/C):
Radius of circle:
```

Enter **I** or **C** and then the radius of the circle.

With the `Edge` option, you are indicating one side of the polygon, not the center point and radius. You are prompted:

```
First endpoint of edge:
Second endpoint of edge:
```

AutoCAD is looking for two points to define one side of the polygon.

PRPLOT

Sends a plot to a printer that accepts graphics information.

Syntax

```
Command: PRPLOT
What to plot — Display, Extents,
    Limits, View, or Window <D>:
```

Description

See the options for the PLOT command.

PURGE

Cleans up the drawing database by removing unused entities.

Syntax

```
Command: PURGE
Purge unused Blocks/LAyers/LTypes/
    SHapes/STyles/All:
```

Description

Unused Blocks, LAyers, LTypes, SHapes, and STyles can be purged. All searches the database for all unused, named objects and presents them for purging.

This command must be used before you make any changes to the database (including adding entities to or removing them from the database).

Layer 0, the continuous linetype, and the standard text style are basic to the drawing and cannot be purged.

QTEXT

Replaces text with a box.

Syntax

```
Command: QTEXT
ON/OFF <current>:
```

Description

QTEXT is a time-saver for large drawings with a great deal of text. When QTEXT replaces the text with a box, the text is still in the database but does not regenerate on-screen.

QUIT

Ends the editing session and returns to the Main Menu without saving changes to the drawing.

Syntax

```
Command: QUIT
Really want to discard all changes
to drawing?
```

Description

Similar in purpose to the END command, this is the way to end a drawing and return to the main AutoCAD menu.

RADIUS

Provides radius dimensions for circles and arcs.

Syntax

```
DIM: RADIUS
Select arc or circle:
Dimension text <measured radius>:
Text does not fit. Enter leader length
    for text:
```

Description

This dimensioning command is available only from the Dim: prompt. See the descriptions for DIM and DIM1 for information about dimensioning.

The location of the dimension is dependent on where you select the entity. If you need to modify the dimension, you can STRETCH, CHANGE, or EXPLODE it.

REDEFINE

Allows you to reset, to its original definition, a standard AutoCAD command that has been defined with a LISP routine.

Syntax

```
Command: REDEFINE
Command name:
```

Description

Enter the name of the command that has been defined to a LISP routine. The command will be reset to its original definition.

REDO

Reverses an UNDO command.

Syntax

```
Command: REDO
```

Description

This command must be used immediately after the U or UNDO command; otherwise, it will not work.

'REDRAW

Redraws entities in the current viewport.

Syntax

```
Command: REDRAW
```

Description

REDRAW can also be used transparently; simply put an apostrophe (') before the command at any prompt.

This command can also be used from the Dim: prompt. See the descriptions for DIM and DIM1 for information about dimensioning.

'REDRAWALL

Redraws all the viewports at one time.

Syntax

Command: REDRAWALL

REGEN

Regenerates the drawing and redraws the current viewport.

Syntax

Command: REGEN

Description

When this command is issued, AutoCAD reads the entire entity database and calculates a new drawing. Using this command may take a while if a large number of are entities in your drawing.

REGENALL

Regenerates all viewports.

Syntax

    Command: REGENALL

REGENAUTO

Limits automatic regeneration.

Syntax

    Command: REGENAUTO
    ON/OFF:

Description

ON enables automatic regeneration; OFF disables automatic regeneration (AutoCAD will ask whether regeneration should occur).

RENAME

Renames entities.

Syntax

    Command: RENAME
    Block/LAyer/LType/Style/Ucs/VIew/
        VPort:
    Old (object) name:
    New (object) name:

Description

At the Block/LAyer/LType/Style/Ucs/VIew/ VPort: prompt, enter the type of entity you want to rename. Then enter the current name at the Old (object) name: prompt and the new name at the New (object) name: prompt.

'RESUME

Continues an interrupted script file.

Syntax

```
Command: RESUME
```

Description

Type the command *without* the apostrophe at the
`Command:` prompt, or type it *with* an apostrophe at
any other prompt for the interrupted script to continue.

REVSURF

Generates a surface of revolution by rotating an outline
around an axis.

Syntax

```
Command: REVSURF
Select path curve:
Select axis of revolution:
Start angle <0>:
Included angle (+=ccw, -=cw) <Full
    circle>:
```

Description

`Select path curve:` prompts for the outline of
the object you are drawing, which can be a line, arc,
circle, two-dimensional polyline, or three-dimensional
polyline. This is the N direction of the resulting mesh.

`Select axis of revolution:` prompts for the
axis around which the path curve is revolved. This axis,
which can be a line or an open polyline, is the M
direction of the resulting mesh.

Start angle <0>: allows you to begin the surface at an offset from the defined path curve.

Included angle (+=ccw, -=cw) <full circle>: specifies how far the entities are rotated around the axis.

ROTATE

Rotates the entities in your drawing.

Syntax

```
Command: ROTATE
Select objects:
Base point:
<Rotation angle>/Reference:
```

Description

Select objects: prompts for the point around which the entities will rotate.

Base point: prompts for the base point.

<Rotation angle> prompts for the rotation angle.

Reference: allows you to reference an entity in the drawing as the current angle and then tell AutoCAD the new rotation. To do this, indicate the ends of the source entity, using OSNAP modes if necessary. Then type the angle to which you want the entities rotated.

ROTATED

Sets a rotation angle for the dimension line.

Syntax

```
DIM: ROTATED
Dimension line angle <0>:
First extension line origin or RETURN
    to select:
Second extension line origin:
Dimension line location:
Dimension text <1.19>:
```

Description

This dimensioning command is available only from the Dim: prompt. See the descriptions for DIM and DIM1 for information about dimensioning.

If the part you are dimensioning is not horizontal or vertical, and you cannot align the dimension, use the ROTATED linear dimension.

RSCRIPT

Reruns a script file.

Syntax

```
Command: RSCRIPT
```

Description

Similar in purpose to the SCRIPT command, this is the way to run a script file an additional time from within the drawing editor.

RULESURF

Creates a ruled surface between two curves, lines, points, arcs, circles, and polylines.

Syntax

```
Command: RULESURF
Select first defining curve:
Select second defining curve:
```

Description

If one of the boundaries is closed, the other must be closed also. AutoCAD starts the surface from the endpoint of the entity nearest the point used to select the entity. With circles, the start is 0 degrees; with polygons, the start is the first vertex.

SAVE

Saves the changes you have made to the drawing, without returning to the Main Menu.

Syntax

```
Command: SAVE
```

Description

It is a good idea to save your work every 10 to 20 minutes, depending on how much time you could afford to spend reconstructing a drawing if you should "lose" the drawing for some reason.

SCALE

Scales what you have drawn.

Syntax

```
Command: SCALE
Select objects:
```

```
Base point:
<Scale factor>/Reference:
```

Description

If you want the finished drawing to be at a particular scale, you can draw at full scale and then use the SCALE command to scale your drawing up or down. You need a base point, and you can either indicate the scale factor or reference part of the object.

At the `Select objects:` prompt, select the entities you want scaled.

`Base point` is the point "from" which the entities will be scaled. If the base point is inside or on the object, the entity will change size at its present location. If the base point is outside the object, the object will move from its original location in accordance with the scale factor.

`<Scale factor>` is looking for a relative scale factor. All selected entities are multiplied by this factor. A factor of less than one shrinks the entities, whereas a factor greater than one increases the size of the entities.

`Reference:` allows you to reference the length of an entity to indicate the new length. All other entities indicated will change size according to the scale generated by the reference.

SCRIPT

Runs script files inside the Drawing Editor.

Syntax

```
Command: SCRIPT
Script file <default>:
```

Description

This is the way to run a script file from within the
Drawing Editor. To run the same script file again, use
the RSCRIPT command.

SELECT

Creates a selection set for use in subsequent commands.

Syntax

```
Command: SELECT
Select objects:
Select objects:
```

'SETVAR

Accesses system variables.

Syntax

```
Command: 'SETVAR
Variable name or ?:
```

SH

Allows a partial shell to the operating system.

Syntax

```
Command: SH
DOS command:
```

Description

The SH command allows you to execute only one command at the system level and then returns you to AutoCAD.

SHAPE

Inserts shapes in the drawing.

Syntax

```
Command: SHAPE
Starting point:
Height <1.0>:
Rotation angle <0.0>:
```

Description

The Starting point: prompt is looking for a location at which to insert the shape. This point corresponds to the first vector in the shape definition.

Height <1.0>: is used to scale the shape.

Rotation angle <0.0>:. The shape can be rotated at a given angle.

You must LOAD shape files before you can use the shapes. Type **LOAD**, press Return, and type the name of the file you want to load. You can use the question mark (?) to list available shape file names.

SHELL

Provides full access to the operating system level.

Syntax

```
Command: SHELL
DOS command:
```

Description

At the DOS Command: prompt, you may execute one command, or you may press Return to get to the system level. At the system level, you can execute as many commands as you want (even other programs). Return to AutoCAD by typing **EXIT** at the DOS prompt.

SKETCH

Allows freehand drawing.

Syntax

```
Command: SKETCH
Record increment <current>:
Sketch. Pen  eXit  Quit  Record
    Erase  Connect
```

Description

To select an option while you are in Sketch mode, all you need to do is type the capitalized letter. You do not need to press Return.

AutoCAD sketches with line or polyline segments. Record increment is the length of these segments. Both SNAP and ORTHO modes affect the way segments are drawn.

The Pen option is a toggle that alternately raises or lowers the pen. If the pen is up, you can move the cursor on the screen without drawing. When the pen is down, AutoCAD draws as the cursor moves.

eXit records the segments permanently and ends Sketch mode.

Quit ends Sketch mode without saving any of the work.

Record saves the segments without exiting.

Erase erases segments as you backtrack through the drawing.

Connect connects new segments to existing segments. Make sure that the pen is up, position the cursor next to an existing segment, and then type **C**.

Sketch is not an option. It is merely a label indicating that you are working in Sketch mode.

SNAP

Provides an invisible grid into which you lock.

Syntax

Command: SNAP
Snap spacing or ON/OFF/Aspect/Rotate/
    Style <current>:

Description

Snap spacing is the default. Just like the GRID command, Snap spacing will set both the X and Y values. Simply type the values you want, and press Return. Values may be as large or as small as needed in the drawing.

SNAP is a toggle. You can turn it on and off from the command (with the ON and OFF options) or by pressing one of the function keys (F9 on IBM® and compatible machines).

Aspect sets the X and Y spacings to different values. You are prompted first for the X value and then for the Y value.

Rotate. If you need to draw at an angle other than horizontal, you can rotate the grid and snap to accommodate. Rotate affects both the visible grid and the invisible snap mode. You are prompted for a base point, around which the grid will be rotated. If you want to align the point with an entity, indicate the entity for the rotation angle. Otherwise, it is a good idea to leave the base point at 0,0.

Style allows you to choose between standard drawing mode (the default) or isometric mode.

Snap mode can be toggled on and off inside commands as you are working. You can toggle snap on and start to draw, then toggle snap off while still in the command. Snap mode is used also when you need a rigid area in which to draw.

Snap mode and grid mode can be compared to using graph paper in your drawings. You can choose to stay on the graph lines or draw between the lines. This is true of both the snap and grid modes.

If you magnify your drawing, the snap setting remains the same. You may need to change the setting when you are doing detail work. Changes in the snap setting do not affect entities already in the drawing. The changes affect only the entities or processes that will happen after the changes are made.

SOLID

Draws solid rectilinear and triangular areas.

Syntax

```
Command: SOLID
First point:
Second point:
Third point:
Fourth point:
```

```
Third point:
Fourth point:
```

Description

To draw solids, you indicate the corners of the area. It is important to indicate the corners correctly to achieve the shape you want. You may indicate three or four corners.

To obtain a rectilinear solid, the points must be arranged so that the first and third points lie on the same edge. If you indicate the points in a clockwise or counterclockwise direction, you will get a bow tie.

If you are drawing only a four-point solid, press Return when you are prompted the second time for the `Third point:`. If you are drawing a three-point solid, press Return at the `Fourth point:` prompt. You will still be prompted for the continuation for the command. If you use the continuation, the solids will be connected.

STATUS

Displays drawing information.

Syntax

`Command:` STATUS

Description

STATUS tells you what your toggles read, what your drawing extents and limits are, how much disk space is available, and how much I/O page space is available.

This command is also available from the `Dim:` prompt. When it is used in the dimensioning mode, the result is a list of dimensioning variables, along with their current settings, displayed on the screen. If there are more

variables than will fit on the screen at one time, press
Return to see the rest of the list. See the descriptions for
DIM and DIM1 for information about dimensioning.

STRETCH

Changes entities while retaining connections with other
entities or points.

Syntax

```
Command: STRETCH
Select objects to stretch by window...
Select objects:
Base point:
New point:
```

Description

The first selection must be made by a window (window
or crossing). Subsequent selections may be made by
pointing. Another window selection will negate the first
window selection.

With STRETCH you can "stretch" entities to make
them smaller or larger, or you can realign those entities
in any way you want.

STYLE

Loads text fonts into your drawing.

Syntax

```
Command: STYLE
```

```
Text style name (or ?) <current>:
Font file <default>:
Height <default>:
Width factor <default>:
Obliquing angle <default>:
Backwards? <Y/N>:
Upside-down? <Y/N>:
Vertical? <Y/N>:
(name) is now the current text style.
```

Description

In addition to allowing the loading of text fonts, this command is also available from the Dim: prompt. See the descriptions for DIM and DIM1 for information about dimensioning.

TABLET

Allows you to turn the tablet on and off, calibrate the tablet for digitizing drawings, or configure the tablet for a menu.

Syntax

```
Command: TABLET
Option (ON/OFF/CAL/CFG):
```

Description

ON returns the tablet to menu use after it has been turned off. OFF turns off the tablet menu and allows you to use the entire tablet area for digitizing. Use the OFF option before calibrating.

CAL allows you to calibrate the tablet to a given paper drawing for the purpose of digitizing the paper drawing into AutoCAD. You are prompted for the following:

```
Digitize first known point:
Enter coordinates for first point:
```

```
Digitize second known point:
Enter coordinates for second point:
```

Secure the paper drawing to the digitizing tablet so that no movement will occur. On the drawing, select two points that you know, and decide what coordinates those two points should have in AutoCAD. These are your first and second points and define the scale of the drawing.

CFG allows you to configure the tablet for different menu areas when you switch between menus. If the menus are defined with the same areas and the same number of squares in each area, you do not need to reconfigure the tablet. You are prompted for the following:

```
Enter number of tablet menus desired
    (0-4) <default>:
Digitize upper left corner of menu
    area n:
Digitize lower left corner of menu
    area n:
Digitize lower right corner of menu
    area n:
Digitize lower left corner of screen
    pointing area:
Digitize upper right corner of
    screen pointing area:
```

n represents the number of the particular tablet area you are defining. If you make a mistake defining one of the corners, you must execute the command again. The screen pointing area that is specified includes the area used for the screen menu, which can be reached through the tablet or other pointing device.

TABSURF

Creates a tabulated surface with a path and a direction vector.

Syntax

```
Command: TABSURF
Select path curve:
Select direction vector:
```

Description

Select Path curve: is used to define the surface. Lines, arcs, circles, and polylines may be used.

Select direction vector: is a line or open polyline showing the direction and length of the surface.

TEXT

Places text in your drawing.

Syntax

```
Command: TEXT
Start point or Align/Center/Fit/
    Middle/Right/Style:
```

Description

Start point is the default for the TEXT command. AutoCAD is looking for the starting point for the text you will insert. The text you enter will be left-justified.

Align prompts for a start point and an ending point for your text. The overall size of the text you enter will be adjusted so that it prints between the two points.

Center centers the text. You are prompted for the center point for the text.

Fit is similar to the Align option. You are prompted for a starting point and an ending point for the text, and for a height. AutoCAD will adjust the width of the text to fit between the two points.

`Middle` is similar to `Center`. The difference is that `Middle` centers text both horizontally and vertically around the point. AutoCAD prompts for a middle point.

`Right` right-justifies your text. You are prompted for an endpoint for the text.

`Style` allows you to switch between the loaded text fonts. To load a text font, see the STYLE command.

If you press Return at this prompt, AutoCAD will prompt you for text. This new text is placed below the last text entered and retains all the parameters of the last text including font, height, rotation, and color.

After you respond to the preceding prompt, you will either be prompted for the endpoints of the base line, or you will see the following prompts:

```
Height <current>:
Rotation <current>:
Text:
```

Spaces are allowed for the text that you input. When you finish typing text, press Return.

The default text font (called STANDARD) is used unless other fonts have been loaded with the STYLE command. There are special characters you can insert with your text. These characters are embedded in the text and need codes to activate them.

The following table shows the codes and the special characters they activate:

Code	_Character_
%%o	Overscore
%%u	Underscore
%%d	Degrees symbol
%%p	Plus/minus symbol
%%c	Circle diameter
%%%	Percent sign
%%nnn	ASCII character code _nnn_

After text has been inserted in the drawing, use the CHANGE command to change it.

'TEXTSCR

Flips to the text screen on a single-screen system.

Syntax

```
Command: 'TEXTSCR
```

Description

The opposite of the GRAPHSCR command, this
command switches from the graphics to the text screen.
You can also use the F1 key to do the same task.

TIME

Keeps track of time spent in a drawing.

Syntax

```
Command: TIME
```

Description

When you enter this command, AutoCAD responds
with a display similar to the following (with values
displayed to the right side of each items):

```
Current time:
Drawing created:
Drawing last updated:
Time in drawing editor:
Elapsed timer:
Timer on.

Display/ON/OFF/Reset:
```

Display redisplays the time. ON turns on the timer;
OFF turns off the timer. Reset causes the time to be
reset to 0.

`Drawing created:` is the date and time the current drawing was created.

`Drawing last updated:` is the last time you updated the current file.

`Time in drawing editor:` is the total time you have spent in the Drawing Editor with this drawing.

`Elapsed timer:` is the time you have spent in the Drawing Editor during the current session.

TRACE

Draws a line of a specific width.

Syntax

```
Command: TRACE
Trace width:
From point:
To point:
To point:
```

Description

An outmoded AutoCAD command that allows the drawing of primitive lines with a specific width.

TRIM

Trims entities back to a boundary.

Syntax

```
Command: TRIM
Select cutting edge(s)...
Select object:
```

Description

The cutting edges are the boundaries to which you are trimming. When all the boundaries have been selected, you are prompted:

```
Select object to trim:
```

Reverses the effect of the most recent command.

Syntax

```
Command: U
```

UCS

Defines or modifies User Coordinate Systems.

Syntax

```
Command: UCS
Origin/ZAxis/3point/Entity/View/X/Y/Z/
    Prev/Restore/Save/Del/?/<World>:
```

Description

Origin defines a new UCS by moving the origin of the current UCS. The orientation of the axis remains the same.

ZAxis defines a new UCS using an origin and a point indicating the positive Z axis. You are prompted:

```
Origin point <0,0,0>:
Point on positive portion of the Z
    axis <default>:
```

3point defines a new UCS with three points: origin,
positive X axis, and positive Y axis. OSNAP modes can
be used to indicate a UCS that corresponds to entities in
the drawing. You are prompted:

```
Origin point <0,0,0>:
Point on positive portion of the X
   axis <current>:
Point on positive-Y portion of the
   UCS X-Y plane <current>:
```

The three points must not form a straight line.

Entity defines a new UCS using an existing entity.
The X-Y plane is parallel to the X-Y plane that was in
effect when the entity was drawn and has the same Z
direction as that of the indicated entity. The entity must
be indicated by pointing. The following list describes
the process of creating the UCS from each type of
entity:

❏ **Arc**. The center becomes the origin; the X axis
    passes through the point on the arc closest to the
    pick point.

❏ **Circle**. Same as arc.

❏ **Dimension**. The insertion point is the origin; the X
    axis is parallel to the UCS of the dimension.

❏ **Line**. The endpoint nearest the pick point is the
    new origin; the Y axis is the other end of the line
    segment indicated.

❏ **Point**. The origin is the point; the X axis is derived
    arbitrarily.

❏ **Polyline and Mesh**. The start point is the new
    origin; the X axis lies from the origin to the next
    vertex.

❏ **Solid**. The first point of solid is the origin; the X
    axis is on the line between the first and second
    points.

❏ **Trace.** The first point is the origin; the X axis lies
    along the center of the trace.

❑ **3D Face**. The first point is the origin; the X axis is from the first two points; and the positive Y side is from the first and fourth points.

❑ **Shape**, **text**, **block**. The origin is the insertion point; the X axis is defined by the rotation.

View defines a new UCS whose Z axis is parallel to the direction of view—that is, perpendicular to the current view.

X/Y/Z rotates the current UCS around the specified axis. You are prompted for the rotation around the axis you indicate.

Previous takes you back to the UCS in which you last worked.

Restore restores a saved UCS.

Save saves the current UCS. You are prompted for a name; the standard conventions apply.

Delete removes the specified UCS from the list. You are prompted for the name of the UCS to delete.

? lists the UCSs that are saved.

World sets the current coordinate system to the World Coordinate System.

UCSICON

Controls the User Coordinate System icon that appears at the bottom of the drawing in Release 10.

Syntax

```
Command: UCSICON
All/Noorigin/ORigin <current>:
```

Description

All activates the icon change in all viewports, not just the current port.

Noorigin (the default) displays the icon at all times in the screen's lower left corner.

ORigin displays the icon at the origin of the current UCS.

OFF turns off the icon; ON turns on the icon.

UNDEFINE

Allows advanced programmers to define standard AutoCAD commands with a new definition.

Syntax

Command: UNDEFINE
Command name:

Description

The indicated command will be defined to the LISP routine currently bearing the command name.

UNDO

Reverses the effect of previous commands and provides control over the undo feature.

Syntax

Command: UNDO
Auto/Back/Control/End/Group/Mark/
    <Number>:

Description

Number is the default. You can enter the number of commands you want undone at this time. If you are stepping back through your database to a particular point but are not sure how far back it is, undo a specific number of commands at a time.

Auto prompts ON/OFF. This is the part of UNDO that controls how menu selections and other multiple commands are handled. If Auto is on, the menu selections are treated as one command.

Group starts the grouping process. When you tell AutoCAD to "open" a group, the next commands you execute become part of that group. When you have entered all the commands you want in that group, you must End the group.

End ends the grouping process. If you start the grouping process, you must end that process. When commands have been grouped together, they are undone with one UNDO command.

Mark allows you to mark a place in your undo information to return to through the UNDO command. You can mark more than one place at a time. When you go back to that mark, the mark is removed. If you want to keep a mark there, you mark the place again. By marking the information, you can experiment in your drawing without worrying about getting back to a particular spot.

Back takes you back to the mark you placed in the undo information. If there are no marks in the undo information, AutoCAD will undo to the beginning of the editing session.

Control allows you to limit the UNDO and U commands. AutoCAD prompts you

    All/None/One:

All is the default, allowing you all of the different UNDO functions. None disables the command, and

One allows one undo at a time. Both None and One free any disk space used for storing previous UNDOs.

UNDO is also available from the Dim: prompt. If used while in dimensioning mode, UNDO undoes the last dimension inserted in the drawing. See the descriptions for DIM and DIM1 for information on dimensioning.

UNITS

Sets the display format and precision of your drawing units.

Syntax

Command: UNITS

Description

When using this command, AutoCAD displays:

```
System of units:   (Examples)
1. Scientific      1.55E+01
2. Decimal         15.50
3. Engineering     1'-3.50"
4. Architectural   1'-3 1/2"
5. Fractional      15 1/2
Enter choice, 1 to 5 <2>:
```

The main type of unit is determined here. The Fractional selection will display units in whole and fraction parts. If this system of units is selected, AutoCAD makes no assumption about whether the units being used are inches or millimeters. The following prompt appears for selections 1, 2, or 3:

```
Number of digits to right of decimal
    point (0 to 8) <default>:
```

The following prompt appears for selections 4 or 5:

```
Denominator of smallest fraction to
    display (1, 2, 4, 8, 16, 32, or
    64) <default>:
```

Next, you are prompted for angle format:

```
System of angle measure:
1. Decimal degrees    42.5
2. Degrees/minutes/seconds
   42d30'0.00"
3. Grads 47.2222g
4. Radians  0.7418r
5. Surveyor's units    N 47d30'0" E

Enter choice, 1 to 5 <default>:
```

When you work with Surveyor's units, the display will be

```
N or S    angle    E or W
```

The angle is input the same as Degrees/minutes/seconds. If the angle you are working with lies on a compass point, simply identify the compass point. For example, 0 degrees would be equivalent to E in Surveyor's units.

The precision of the angle measurement is selected next. The prompt is

```
Number of fractional places for
    display of angles (0 to 8)<>:
```

Next, you are prompted for the direction of angle 0. The default in AutoCAD is for angle 0 to be at "3 o'clock," and the angles to be figured counterclockwise. The next prompt in the UNITS command follows:

```
Direction for angle 0:
    East    3 o'clock = 0
    North 12 o'clock = 90
    West    9 o'clock = 180
    South   6 o'clock = 270
Enter direction for angle 0
    <default>:
```

If you want to specify an angle other than those listed here, and you have a single-screen system, use the F1 function key to flip to the graphics screen. Then indicate the angle with two points. A word of caution: if you indicate an angle in this manner, remember what you have done; you may become easily confused with a nonstandard angle as your 0 angle.

The last prompt in the UNITS command controls the direction of angles. By default, AutoCAD works counterclockwise. You can work clockwise or counter-clockwise. The prompt follows:

```
Do you want angles measured
    clockwise? <N>:
```

UPDATE

Updates dimensions to current dimension variables.

Syntax
```
DIM: UPDATE
Select objects:
```

Description
This dimensioning command is available only from the Dim: prompt. See the descriptions for DIM and DIM1 for information about dimensioning.

VERTICAL

Gives the vertical (Y) distance from one point to the next.

Syntax

```
DIM: VERTICAL
First extension line origin or Return
    to select:
Second extension line origin:
Dimension line location:
Dimension text <value>:
```

Description

This dimensioning command is available only from the
Dim: prompt. See the descriptions for DIM and DIM1
for information about dimensioning.

'VIEW

Creates views of zoomed work areas.

Syntax

```
Command: VIEW
?/Delete/Restore/Save/Window:
View name:
```

Description

? lists all the views that currently exist in the drawing.

Delete removes from the list the reference for the
specified view.

Restore causes the view to be restored to the screen
after it has been defined. Restore is used to flip
between the views.

Save saves whatever is currently on-screen as a view.
You are prompted for a view name, which can be 31
characters long and may contain letters, numbers,
dollar signs ($), hyphens (-), and underscores (_). You
reference the view by its view name.

Window allows you to make several views without zooming in on a view. You put a window around the area you want to be the view.

VIEWPORTS or VPORTS

Controls the number of viewports on the screen.

Syntax

```
Command: VPORTS
Save/Restore/Delete/Join/Off/?/2/
    <3>/4:
```

Description

Save saves the current viewport configuration for future use. You are not limited to the number of viewports that can be saved. You are prompted for the name of the viewports; standard requirements apply to the name.

Restore restores a saved viewport.

Delete deletes a saved viewport configuration.

Join merges two adjacent viewports into one larger viewport. The resulting viewport is inherited from the dominant viewport. You are prompted:

```
Select dominant viewport <current>:
Select viewport to merge:
```

Off returns you to single viewport (normal) viewing.

? lists the viewports currently saved.

2,3,4 allows you to define 2, 3, or 4 viewports in a configuration of your choice. 2 viewports are defined with either a vertical or horizontal configuration. 3 viewports are defined with one large port next to 2 small ports. 4 viewports divides the screen into 4 equal areas.

If you use the pull-down menus for VPORT, choosing the configuration is easier.

VIEWRES

Controls AutoCAD's fast regeneration and the resolution of circles and arcs as they are drawn and represented.

Syntax

```
Command: VIEWRES
Do you want fast zooms? <Y>:
Enter circle zoom percent <1-20000)
    <100>:
```

Description

If you respond with **Y** to the first prompt, AutoCAD will allow fast regenerations. The circle zoom percent is the value that determines the resolution of circles and arcs in AutoCAD. The default is 100.

VPOINT

Allows you to see your drawing in three dimensions.

Syntax

```
Command: VPOINT
Rotate/<View point> <current>:
```

Description

The default view point is 0,0,1. When you want to return to the plan view of your drawing, type those coordinates at the prompt. You can use the pull-down menus also to determine your view point.

VSLIDE

Allows you to view previously created slides.

Syntax

```
Command: VSLIDE
Slide file <default>:
```

Description

To view slides from a library, respond as follows:

```
Command: VSLIDE
Slide file: library(slide)
```

WBLOCK

Creates blocks that can be used in all drawings.

Syntax

```
Command: WBLOCK
File name:
Block name:
```

Description

`File name.` AutoCAD wants to know the name of the file it is creating to hold the block. The file name must comply with DOS standards.

`Block name.` AutoCAD wants to know the name of the block to write to the file. If the block does not exist yet, press Return. You will be prompted with the standard BLOCK creation prompts. If the block and the file have the same name, you may type the shorthand character—the equal sign (=). If the entire drawing is being written out, use the asterisk (*). Otherwise, type the name of the block to be written to file.

You can go into the WBLOCK files by selecting 2 from the Main Menu.

'ZOOM

Allows you to magnify or condense parts of the drawing.

Syntax

```
Command: ZOOM
All/Center/Dynamic/Extents/Left/
    Previous/Window/<Scale(X)>:
```

Description

All returns you to your drawing limits or the extents, whichever is larger.

Center allows you to identify a new center point for the screen and then enter the height. This height is the factor that determines the zoom scale.

Dynamic causes a new screen to appear on the monitor.

Extents. The extents of the drawing are the precise area in which you have drawn. The X and Y values make up the drawing extents. Extents pulls all entities in the drawing onto the screen. This is a good way to see whether any "rogue entities" are floating around in the drawing.

Left allows you to set a new lower left corner and height.

Previous returns you to the previous screen.

Window allows you to place a window around the area in which you want to work.

Scale allows you to zoom by a scale factor.

3DFACE

Draws three-dimensional flat planes.

Syntax

```
Command: 3DFACE
First point:
Second point:
Third point:
Fourth point:
Third point:
Fourth point:
```

Description

The 3DFACE drawings are similar to the SOLID
drawings created in the X-Y plane. The prompt
sequence is identical to that for the SOLID command.
The difference is in the point input; the points used to
define the 3DFACE must be indicated either clockwise
or counterclockwise.

3DMESH

Creates a general polygon mesh by specifying the size
of the mesh, in terms of M and N, and the vertices for
the mesh.

Syntax

```
Command: 3DMESH
Mesh M size:
Mesh N size:
Vertex (0,0):
Vertex (x,y):
Vertex (x,y):
Vertex (x,y):
```

Description

M size and N size define how many vertices the mesh will have (M x N vertices).

Vertex. Default vertices correspond to the current UCS and to the M and N sizes. Vertices may be two- or three-dimensional points.

The 3DMESH command, used for specifying arbitrary meshes, is best used in LISP. For easier use of meshes, see RULESURF, TABSURF, REVSURF, and EDGESURF.

3DPOLY

Draws three-dimensional polylines.

Syntax

```
Command: 3DPOLY
From point:
Close/Undo/<Endpoint of line>:
```

Description

From point: is the start of the polyline.

Close closes a polyline with two or more segments.

Undo undoes the last endpoint.

The <Endpoint of line>: option prompts for the next endpoint for the polyline.

Points may be two- or three-dimensional. Use the PEDIT command to edit three-dimensional polylines.

System Variables

This is a complete list of all AutoCAD system variables (including dimensioning variables). Each variable generally has a default, a variable type, and is many times saved with the drawing or in another AutoCAD file. The possible types of AutoCAD variables are:

❑ Integer

❑ Real

❑ Text String

❑ Two-Dimensional Point

❑ Three-Dimensional Point

❑ Toggles On or Off

The description for each variable will indicate the type for the variable. Many of the AutoCAD variables are used internally by different AutoCAD commands, and thus are considered read-only (they cannot be changed directly). Variables that are not read-only can be changed with the SETVAR command.

ACADPREFIX

If you specified a directory other than the AutoCAD directory for your drawing, that information is stored here. This string variable is read-only.

ACADVER

The current release of AutoCAD. If you are using Release 10, the default should be 10. This string variable is read-only.

AFLAGS

Contains information that determines whether attributes are

1	invisible
2	constant
3	verify
4	preset

This integer variable defaults to 0 and is set when the ATTDEF command is first executed.

ANGBASE

Defaults to 3 o'clock. Contains the direction for angle 0. This real number variable is used to calculate all angles in AutoCAD. It is saved with the AutoCAD drawing.

ANGDIR

This integer variable defines whether angles entered in AutoCAD will default to clockwise (0) or counter-clockwise (1). Counterclockwise is the default. This variable is saved with the AutoCAD drawing.

APERTURE

Defines OSNAP target (aperture) height. This integer variable defaults to 10 and is set with APERTURE command. It is saved in the ACAD.CFG configuration file.

AREA

This real number variable holds value of the true area from the most recent of any of these commands: AREA, LIST, or DBLIST. This variable is read-only and defaults to 0.

ATTDIA

This integer variable controls whether the INSERT command displays a dialogue box for any attributes defined with a given block. A value of 1 displays dialogue box; 0 (the default) does not. This variable is saved with the AutoCAD drawing.

ATTMODE

This integer variable holds value of ATTDISP command. 0 = off, 1 (the default) = normal, 2 = on. This variable is saved with the AutoCAD drawing.

ATTREQ

Controls whether all attributes are set to their defaults (a value of 0) or whether you are prompted for attributes (a value of 1). This integer variable defaults to 1 and is saved with the AutoCAD drawing.

AUNITS

This integer variable holds angular units for the UNITS command:

0	decimal degrees
1	degrees/minutes/seconds
2	grads
3	radians
4	surveyors units.

This variable defaults to 0 and is saved with the AutoCAD drawing.

AUPREC

An integer indicating the precision of angular units. Defaults to 0; saved with the AutoCAD drawing.

AXISMODE

Controls axis display (AXIS command). 0 (the default) = off, 1 = on. This integer variable is saved with the AutoCAD drawing.

AXISUNIT

This two-dimensional point holds the spacing of tick marks for the AXIS command. This variable defaults to 0,0 and is saved with the AutoCAD drawing. A change to this variable is not reflected in the displayed grid and axis until a redraw operation is performed.

BACKZ

The offset for back clipping plane, set with DVIEW command. The units are drawing units. The distance from target to clipping plane can be found by using the following formula: camera-to-target distance - BACKZ.

This real number variable is read-only. It is saved with the AutoCAD drawing.

BLIPMODE
This variable is a toggle that controls whether blips appear on-screen. Set with BLIPMODE command, the default is 1 (ON). This variable is saved with the AutoCAD drawing.

CDATE
This real number variable holds the current date and time for the drawing. This variable is read-only.

CECOLOR
Holds color with which you are currently drawing (defaults to BYLAYER). This string variable is read-only and is saved with the AutoCAD drawing.

CELTYPE
Holds linetype with which you are currently drawing (defaults to BYLAYER). This string variable is read-only. This variable is saved with the AutoCAD drawing.

CHAMFERA
A real number (default of 0) that holds the first chamfer distance. This variable is saved with the AutoCAD drawing.

CHAMFERB
A real number (default of 0) that holds the second chamfer distance. This variable is saved with the AutoCAD drawing.

CLAYER
A text string indicating the name of the current layer. This variable is read-only and is saved with the AutoCAD drawing.

CMDECHO

An integer variable that indicates whether commands are echoed to (appear on) the screen as you use them. Used for programming purposes. Defaults to 1.

COORDS

Controls coordinate display at top of screen. If 0 (default), updated only when you pick a point; if 1, updated as crosshairs travel around screen. This integer variable is saved with the AutoCAD drawing.

CVPORT

Holds identification for current viewport. Defaults to 4; this integer variable is saved with the AutoCAD drawing.

DATE

Holds current Julian calendar date and time for drawing. This real number variable is read-only.

DIMALT

A toggle that controls the generation of alternate dimensions. This variable defaults to 0 (Off) and is saved with the AutoCAD drawing.

DIMALTD

Controls decimal places for alternate dimension value (defaults to 2). This integer variable is saved with the AutoCAD drawing.

DIMALTF

AutoCAD multiplies this real number value (the alternate units scale factor) with the value determined by the current dimension. If DIMALT is on, the alternate value will appear along with the normal value. This variable defaults to 25.4 and is saved with the AutoCAD drawing.

DIMAPOST

A text string that holds the suffix for alternate dimensions. This variable is read-only at the `Command:` prompt; it can be set only at the `Dim:` prompt. This variable is saved with the AutoCAD drawing.

DIMASO

A toggle that controls the generation of associative dimensions. If on (1; the default), dimensions are associative; if off (0), dimensions are normal. This variable is saved with the AutoCAD drawing.

DIMASZ

A real number indicating the dimensioning arrow size. AutoCAD uses this size, the size of the text, and a default minimum length for the dimension line to determine whether dimension text will be inside or outside the dimension. This variable defaults to 0.18 and is saved with the AutoCAD drawing.

DIMBLK

If you need an indicator instead of the arrows or tick marks, you can create a block and indicate its name here. This string variable is read-only at the `Command:` prompt; it can be set only at the `Dim:` prompt. This variable is saved with the AutoCAD drawing.

DIMBLK1

If you want one arrow on the dimension line to be different from the other arrow, DIMBLK1 is placed on the end of the dimension line that extends to the first extension line. This string variable is read-only at the `Command:` prompt; it can be set only at the `Dim:` prompt. This variable is saved with the AutoCAD drawing.

DIMBLK2

If you want one arrow on the dimension line to be different from the other, DIMBLK2 is placed on the end of the dimension line that extends to the second extension line. This string variable is read-only at the `Command:` prompt; it can be set only at the `Dim:` prompt. This variable is saved with the AutoCAD drawing.

DIMCEN

Changes size of center mark AutoCAD inserts with the CENTER command. The default is 0.09. The size is the distance from center mark along one of the line segments. This real number variable is saved with the AutoCAD drawing.

DIMDLE2

If you are using tick marks, this real number variable can be used to extend the dimension line past the extension lines. This variable defaults to 0 and is saved with the AutoCAD drawing.

DIMDLI

Controls increment size AutoCAD uses to offset dimensions (default is 0.38) when using BAS and CON. This real number variable is saved with the AutoCAD drawing.

DIMEXE

Controls extension above dimension line of extension lines. If you do not want an extension, change this real number variable from the default of 0.18 to 0. This variable is saved with the AutoCAD drawing.

DIMEXO

Controls extension line offset from origin. If you do not want an offset, set this real number variable from the default of 0.0625 to 0. This variable is saved with the AutoCAD drawing.

DIMLFAC

Sets scale factor for the drawing. The default (1) is to full scale (one drawing inch equals one object inch). If you are drawing in half scale, set this variable to 2; AutoCAD will multiply the measured values by this real number variable. Angular dimensions are not affected. This variable is saved with the AutoCAD drawing.

DIMLIM

A toggle that controls whether limits are generated using the values in DIMTM and DIMTP. The default is Off (0), and the variable is saved with the AutoCAD drawing.

DIMPOST

A string that holds a default suffix for dimension text. You can enter a suffix to be attached to dimensions as they are inserted. This variable is read-only at the `Command:` prompt; it can be set only at the `Dim:` prompt. This variable is saved with the AutoCAD drawing.

DIMRND

A real number that controls rounding for all dimension values you insert. For example, if you set the value to 0.5, all dimensions will be rounded to nearest half unit. The default is 0 and the variable is saved with the AutoCAD drawing.

DIMSAH

A toggle; if set to On (1), AutoCAD uses block names in DIMBLK1 and DIMBLK2 as arrow heads for dimensioning. Default is Off (0). This variable is saved with the AutoCAD drawing.

DIMSCALE

A real number that scales an entire dimension by the same amount. This variable is useful when you are working with either a large or an extremely small drawing. This variable defaults to 1 and is saved with the AutoCAD drawing.

DIMSE1

A toggle that controls suppression of the first extension line. This variable defaults to Off (0) and is saved with the AutoCAD drawing.

DIMSE2

A toggle that controls suppression of the second extension line. This variable defaults to Off (0) and is saved with the AutoCAD drawing.

DIMSHO

When this toggle is On (1), dimension values are updated as a dimension changes. If set to the default (Off, or 0), dimension text will be updated after the change. This variable is saved with the drawing.

DIMSOXD

This toggle suppresses outside-extension dimension lines. This variable defaults to Off (0) and is saved with the AutoCAD drawing.

DIMTAD

This toggle controls placement of dimension text above a dimension line. This variable defaults to Off (0) and is saved with the AutoCAD drawing.

DIMTIH

Draws all text horizontally inside the dimensions (parallel to bottom edge of paper). When this toggle is turned off, text is inserted aligned to dimension line and is readable from bottom or right side of the drawing. The default is On (1). This variable is saved with the AutoCAD drawing.

DIMTIX

This toggle forces dimension text to appear between extension lines, even if dimension line and arrows do not fit. This variable defaults to Off (0) and is saved with the AutoCAD drawing.

DIMTM

A real number (default 0) that sets negative tolerances
for dimensions. This variable is saved with the
AutoCAD drawing.

DIMTOFL

A toggle that forces AutoCAD to draw dimension lines
between extension lines, even if the dimension text is
forced outside. The default is Off (0), and the variable
is saved with the AutoCAD drawing.

DIMTOH

Draws all text horizontally outside the dimensions.
When this toggle is set to Off (0), dimension text is
drawn in alignment with dimension line and is readable
from bottom or right side of page. The default is On
(1). This variable is saved with the AutoCAD drawing.

DIMTOL

A toggle that causes tolerance generation using
tolerance settings defined in DIMTP and DIMTM. The
default is Off (0), and this variable is saved with the
AutoCAD drawing.

DIMTP

A real number (default 0) that defines positive tolerances for dimensions. This variable is saved with the
AutoCAD drawing.

DIMTSZ

A real number (default 0) that sets a size for tick marks.
If you want arrow heads, type **0** for tick mark size. This
variable is saved with the AutoCAD drawing.

DIMTVP

Allows you to place dimension text above or below a
dimension line. AutoCAD uses the calculation
DIMTVP x DIMTXT to place the text. To use this
variable, DIMTAD must be off. If the real number

value of DIMTVP is positive, text is placed above
dimension line; if negative, text is placed below
dimension line. This variable defaults to 0 and is saved
with the AutoCAD drawing.

DIMTXT

A real number that controls text size (default 0.18) for
dimensions. This variable is saved with the AutoCAD
drawing.

DIMZIN

Controls AutoCAD's zero-inch editing feature of
dimensioning when you are working with architectural
units. If 0 (default), zero feet and zero inches not placed
in dimension. If 1, both zero feet and zero inches placed
in dimension. If 2, only zero feet placed in dimension,
and if 3, zero inches are placed in dimension. This
integer variable is saved with the AutoCAD drawing.

DISTANCE

A real number indicating the last value computed by
the DIST command. This variable is read-only.

DRAGMODE

Controls the dragging of entities (default 2). This
integer variable is saved with the AutoCAD drawing.

DRAGP1

Controls speed at which entities being dragged are
redrawn (default 10). This integer variable is saved in
the ACAD.CFG configuration file.

DRAGP2

Controls speed at which entities being dragged are
redrawn (default 25). This integer variable is saved in
the ACAD.CFG configuration file.

DWGNAME

A string containing the name of current drawing. This variable is read-only and is saved with the AutoCAD drawing.

DWGPREFIX

A string containing the path for the current drawing. This variable is read-only.

ELEVATION

A real number representing the value for the current elevation. This variable is saved with the AutoCAD drawing.

EXPERT

An integer variable that controls the issuance of `Are you sure?` prompts as follows:

0 (Default) Issues all prompts normally

1 Suppresses `About to regen, proceed?` and `Really want to turn the current layer off?`;

2 Suppresses preceding prompts and BLOCK's `Block already defined. Redefine it?` and SAVE/WBLOCK's `A drawing with this name already exists. Overwrite it?`;

3 Suppresses preceding prompts and those issued by LINETYPE if you try to load a linetype that is already loaded or create a new linetype in a file that already defines it;

4 Suppresses preceding prompts and those issued by UCS Save and VPORTS Save, if the name you supply already exists.

When a prompt is suppressed by EXPERT, the operation in question is performed as though you had responded **Y** to the prompt. This variable is saved with the AutoCAD drawing.

EXTMAX

A three-dimensional (XYZ) point indicating the upper right coordinate of the area in which you have drawn. This variable is read-only and defaults such that X = -1.0E+20, Y = -1.0E+20, and Z = -1.0E+20. This variable is saved with the AutoCAD drawing.

EXTMIN

A three-dimensional (XYZ) point indicating the lower left coordinate of the area in which you have drawn. This variable is read-only and defaults such that X = 1.0E+20, Y = 1.0E+20, and Z = 1.0E+20. This variable is saved with the AutoCAD drawing.

FILLETRAD

A real number (default 0) indicating the radius used by the FILLET command. This variable is saved with the AutoCAD drawing.

FILLMODE

An integer value (default 1) that controls whether polylines and solids are filled with color. This variable is saved with the AutoCAD drawing.

FLATLAND

Allows you to draw in two-dimensions. Default of 0 allows Release 10 capabilities. This integer variable is saved with the AutoCAD drawing.

FRONTZ

Location of front clipping plane, defined with DVIEW command. This variable defaults to 0 and is read-only. This real number variable is saved with the AutoCAD drawing.

GRIDMODE

Controls whether grid is on or off. The default is off (0). This integer variable is saved with the AutoCAD drawing.

GRIDUNIT

A two-dimensional variable that contains the grid spacing for current grid. This variable defaults to 0,0 and is saved with the AutoCAD drawing. A change to this variable is not reflected in the displayed grid and axis until a redraw operation is performed.

HANDLES

An integer (default 0) used to turn handles on or off. This variable is read-only and is saved with the drawing.

HIGHLIGHT

Controls whether entities selected for a particular operation are highlighted. An integer variable with a default of 1.

INSBASE

A three-dimensional point indicating the insertion base point for the drawing. The default is 0,0,0 in the WCS. This variable is saved with the AutoCAD drawing.

LASTANGLE

A real number representing the end angle of last arc entered, relative to X-Y plane of current UCS. This variable is read-only.

LASTPOINT

A three-dimensional point (default 0,0,0) indicating the last point entered, in UCS coordinates.

LASTPT3D

Same as LASTPOINT.

LENSLENGTH

Length of lens, in millimeters (default 50). Used in perspective viewing, this real number variable is set during the DVIEW command. This variable is read-only and is saved with the AutoCAD drawing.

LIMCHECK

An integer variable that controls the limits-check alarm. This variable defaults to 0 and is saved with the AutoCAD drawing.

LIMMAX

A two-dimensional point representing the upper right drawing limits, in World coordinates. This variable is saved with the AutoCAD drawing.

LIMMIN

A two-dimensional point (default 0,0) representing the lower left drawing limits, in World coordinates. This variable is saved with the AutoCAD drawing.

LTSCALE

A real number (default 1) indicating the global linetype scale factor. This variable is saved with the drawing.

LUNITS

An integer that holds the value set for units with the UNITS command. The default value is 2, and this variable is saved with the AutoCAD drawing.

LUPREC

An integer that signifies the number of decimal places for linear units (default is 4). This variable is saved with the AutoCAD drawing.

MENUECHO

An integer that controls menu echo and prompting. This value represents the sum of the following:

0	(Default) Displays menu items and system prompts
1	Suppresses echo of menu items
2	Suppresses printing of system prompts
4	Ddisables ^P toggle of menu-item echoing.

MENUNAME

A string that holds the name of the menu file currently in use. This variable is read-only but can be set with the MENU command. This variable is saved with the AutoCAD drawing.

MIRRTEXT

An integer that controls whether text is mirrored when the MIRROR command is used. If 0, text will retain its "direction" and be mirrored but readable. This variable defaults to 1 and is saved with the AutoCAD drawing.

ORTHOMODE

Toggle for Ortho mode. This variable defaults to 0 and is saved with the AutoCAD drawing.

OSMODE

Holds values for OSNAP modes currently in use. This integer variable defaults to 0 and is saved with the AutoCAD drawing.

PDMODE

Holds value of point-entity display. This integer variable defaults to 0 and is saved with the drawing.

PDSIZE

A real number that defines point-entity size (default 0). This variable is saved with the AutoCAD drawing.

PERIMETER

A real number representing the perimeter computed by one of the following; AREA, LIST, OR DBLIST. This variable is read-only.

PICKBOX

Object selection target height, in pixels (default 3). This integer variable is saved in ACAD.CFG.

POPUPS

An integer (default 1) that defines whether dialogue boxes, menu bars, pull-down menus, and icon menus are supported. This variable is read-only.

QTEXTMODE

An integer that holds the value for QTEXT command (default 0). This variable is saved with the drawing.

REGENMODE

Holds the integer value for REGENAUTO (default 1). This variable is saved with the AutoCAD drawing.

SCREENSIZE

A two-dimensional point indicating the current view-port size, in pixels. This variable is read-only.

SKETCHINC

A real number (default 0.1) specifying the Sketch mode increment value. Saved with the drawing.

SKPOLY

Determines whether lines or polylines are created during Sketch mode (default 0). This integer variable is saved with the AutoCAD drawing.

SNAPANG

A real number indicating the snap/grid rotation angle for the current viewport. This variable defaults to 0 and is saved with the AutoCAD drawing. A change to this variable is not reflected in the displayed grid and axis until a redraw operation is performed.

SNAPBASE

A two-dimensional value (default 0,0) specifying the snap/grid origin point for the current viewport. This variable is saved with the AutoCAD drawing. A change to this variable is not reflected in the displayed grid and axis until a redraw operation is performed.

SNAPISOPAIR

The isoplane currently in use (default 0). This integer variable is saved with the AutoCAD drawing.

SNAPMODE

Snap mode toggle (default 0). This integer variable is saved with the AutoCAD drawing.

SNAPSTYL

Holds the integer value for SNAP style (standard = 0, isometric = 1). The default is 0, and this variable is saved with the AutoCAD drawing.

SNAPUNIT

A two-dimensional point (default 1,1) indicating the snap spacing. This variable is saved with the AutoCAD drawing. A change to this variable is not reflected in the displayed grid and axis until a redraw operation is performed.

SPLFRAME

An integer value that controls the display of a spline frame. This variable defaults to 0 and is saved with the AutoCAD drawing.

SPLINESEGS

An integer indicating the number of line segments to be generated for each spline patch (default 8). This variable is saved with the AutoCAD drawing.

SPLINETYPE

An integer value controlling the type of spline curve to be generated by PEDIT Spline:

5	Quadratic B-spline
6	(Default) Cubic B-spline

This variable is saved with the AutoCAD drawing.

SURFTAB1

The number of tabulations to be generated for RULESURF and TABSURF; also, mesh density in M direction for REVSURF and EDGESURF. This integer variable defaults to 6 and is saved with the drawing.

SURFTAB2

The mesh density in N direction for REVSURF and EDGESURF. This integer variable defaults to 6 and is saved with the AutoCAD drawing.

SURFTYPE

The type of surface fitting to be performed by PEDIT Smooth:

5	Quadratic B-spline surface
6	(Default) Cubic B-spline surface
8	Bezier surface

This integer variable is saved with the drawing.

SURFU

Holds the integer value for the M-direction density of meshes defined by 3DMESH command. This variable defaults to 6 and is saved with the AutoCAD drawing.

SURFV

Holds the integer value for the N-direction density of meshes defined by 3DMESH command. This variable defaults to 6 and is saved with the AutoCAD drawing.

TARGET

A three-dimensional point (0,0,0) representing the location of the target set with DVIEW command. This variable is read-only and is saved with the drawing.

TDCREATE

A real number representing the time and date of drawing creation. This variable is read-only and is saved with the AutoCAD drawing.

TDINDWG

A real number that represents total editing time. This variable is read-only and is saved with the drawing.

TDUPDATE

A real number representing the time and date of the last update or save. This variable is read-only and is saved with the AutoCAD drawing.

TDUSRTIMER

A real number representing the user elapsed time. This variable is read-only and is saved with the drawing.

TEMPPREFIX

A directory name (text string) configured for placement of temporary files. This variable is read-only.

TEXTEVAL

An integer variable used for programs in AutoLISP.

TEXTSIZE

Default height for new text entities (default of 0.2) drawn with the current text style. This real number variable is saved with the AutoCAD drawing.

TEXTSTYLE

A string containing the name of the current text style. This variable is read-only and is saved with the AutoCAD drawing.

THICKNESS

A real number representing the current three-dimensional thickness (default is 0). This variable is saved with the AutoCAD drawing.

TRACEWID

A real number representing the default trace width (defaults to 0.05). This variable is saved with the AutoCAD drawing.

UCSFOLLOW

If this integer variable is set to 1, automatic viewing of plan view for a new UCS is allowed. The default is 0, and this variable is saved with the AutoCAD drawing.

UCSICON

An integer that controls the location of the UCS icon (default of 1). This variable is saved with the drawing.

UCSNAME

A text string representing the name of the current UCS. This variable is read-only and is saved with the AutoCAD drawing.

UCSORG

A three-dimensional point that holds origin (default of 0,0,0) of the current UCS, in World Coordinates. This variable is read-only and is saved with the drawing.

UCSXDIR

A three-dimensional point that is the X-direction (default 0,0,0) of the current UCS. This variable is read-only and is saved with the AutoCAD drawing.

UCSYDIR

A three-dimensional point that is the Y-direction (default 0,0,0) of the current UCS. This variable is read-only and is saved with the AutoCAD drawing.

USERI1–5

Five integer variables for storage and retrieval of integer values (intended for use by third-party developers). These variables are saved with the drawing.

USERR1–5

Five real number variables for storage and retrieval of real numbers (intended for use by third-party developers). These variables are saved with the drawing.

VIEWCTR

A three-dimensional point (X,Y,Z) representing the center of the view in the current viewport, in UCS coordinates. This variable defaults such that X=7.219, Y=4.5, and Z=0 and is read-only. This variable is saved with the AutoCAD drawing.

VIEWDIR

A three-dimensional point (X,Y,Z) representing the viewing direction of the current viewport, in World Coordinates. This variable is read-only. It defaults to 0,0,1 and is saved with the AutoCAD drawing.

VIEWMODE

The viewing mode for the current viewport. This integer defaults to 0 (Off), but may be set to the sum of the following:

1	Perspective view active
2	Front clipping on
4	Back clipping on
8	UCS follow mode on
16	Front clip not at eye

If on, FRONTZ (the front clipping distance) determines the front clipping plane. If off, FRONTZ is ignored, and the front clipping plane is set to pass through the camera point (vectors behind camera are not displayed). This flag is ignored if front clipping bit (2) is off. This variable is read-only. This variable is saved with the AutoCAD drawing.

VIEWSIZE

A real number representing the height of the view in the current viewport (default of 9), in drawing units. This variable is read-only and is saved with the AutoCAD drawing.

VIEWTWIST

A real number variable used by the DVIEW command. This variable is read-only and is saved with the AutoCAD drawing.

VPOINTX

The real number X component of the current viewport's viewing direction, in World Coordinates. Describes the "camera" point as a three-dimensional offset from the target point. This variable is read-only, defaults to 0, and is saved with the AutoCAD drawing.

VPOINTY

The real number Y component of the current viewport's viewing direction, in World Coordinates. Describes the "camera" point as a three-dimensional offset from the target point. This variable is read-only, defaults to 0, and is saved with the AutoCAD drawing.

VPOINTZ

The real number Z component of the current viewport's viewing direction, in World Coordinates. Describes the "camera" point as a three-dimensional offset from the target point. This variable is read-only, defaults to 1, and is saved with the AutoCAD drawing.

VSMAX

A three-dimensional point representing the upper right corner of the current viewport's "virtual screen," in UCS coordinates. This variable defaults such that X=14.4381, Y=9, and Z=0. It is read-only.

VSMIN

A three-dimensional point (default of 0,0,0) representing the lower left corner of the current viewport's "virtual screen," in UCS coordinates. This variable is read-only.

WORLDUCS

If 1 (the default), the current UCS is the same as the World Coordinate System. If set to 0, it is not. This integer variable is read-only.

WORLDVIEW

Normally, VIEW and VPOINT command input is relative to current UCS (this variable defaults to 0). If this integer variable is set to 1, the current UCS is changed to the World Coordinate System for the duration of a DVIEW or VPOINT command. This variable is read-only and is saved with the drawing.

Response Summary

When you enter a command in AutoCAD, you often are prompted for additional responses or information. This section is useful as a quick reminder of possible responses to the prompts produced when you use AutoCAD commands. If no additional information is included under the command, then there are no additional options available.

APERTURE	*Controls the size of the aperture box in OSNAP modes*

ARC	*Draws an arc segment*
A	Angle
C	Center point
D	Starting direction
E	End point
L	Length of chord
R	Radius
Return	(As reply to Start point) Sets start point and direction at end of last line or arc

AREA	*Calculates the area of an object*
A	Add mode
S	Subtract mode
E	Compute area of circle or polyline
ARRAY	*Makes multiple copies of entities*
P	Polar array
R	Rectangular array
ATTDEF	*Creates an attribute definition that controls various aspects of textual information you assign to a block*
I	Control visibility
C	Control accessibility
V	Control verification
P	Control preset mode
ATTDISP	*Overrides the default visibility setting for all attributes*
ON	Make all attributes visible
OFF	Make all attributes invisible
N	Normal visibility
ATTEDIT	*Allows you to edit attributes*
ATTEXT	*Creates a file that contains attribute information for the current drawing*
CDF	Comma delimited format
SDF	SDF format
DXF	DXF format
E	Select particular entities
AXIS	*Sets up an axis of tick marks on the bottom and right side of the drawing*
ON	Turn on axis
OFF	Turn off axis
S	Set axis to current snap value
A	Change X-Y values
number	Set tick spacing

numberX	Set tick spacing to multiple of snap spacing
BASE	*Creates the insertion point when you want to insert one drawing into another*
BLIPMODE	*Toggles blips on and off*
ON	Turn on marker blips
OFF	Turn off marker blips
BLOCK	*Creates an object from existing entities*
?	List names of defined blocks
BREAK	*Removes parts of an entity or separates an entity into segments*
F	Respecify first point
CHAMFER	*Trims or extends two lines until specified distances are met and then connects the lines with a line segment*
D	Set distances
P	Chamfer polyline
CHANGE	*Modifies entities*
P	Change Properties
C	Change Color
E	Change Elevation
LA	Change Layer
LT	Change Linetype
T	Change Thickness
CHPROP	*Modifies the properties of entities*
C	Change Color
LA	Change Layer
LT	Change Linetype
T	Change Thickness

CIRCLE	*Draws a circle*
2P	Specify 2 endpoints of diameter
3P	Specify 3 points on circumference
D	Enter diameter instead of radius
TTR	Specify two tangent points and radius
COLOR	*Sets the color for drawing entities*
number	Entity color number
name	Entity color name
BYBLOCK	Floating entity color
BYLAYER	Match layer's color
COPY	*Copies selected objects*
M	Make multiple copies
DBLIST	*Lists information about all the entities in a drawing*
DDATTE	*Allows attribute editing by means of a dialogue box*
'DDEMODES	*Allows layer-setting changes by means of a dialogue box*
'DDLMODES	*Changes layer properties by means of a dialogue box*
'DDRMODES	*Sets drawing aids by means of a dialogue box*
DDUCS	*Controls the User Coordinate System by means of a dialogue box*
DELAY	*Delays execution of the next command in a script*
DIM, DIM1	*Sets dimensioning mode*

DIST	*Calculates the distance between two points*
DIVIDE	*Divides the entity into equal parts*
B	Use specified block as marker
DONUT	*Inserts a solid filled ring in the drawing*
DOUGHNUT	*Same as DONUT*
DRAGMODE	*Modifies dragging*
ON	Turn on dragmode
OFF	Turn off dragmode
A	Auto mode
DTEXT	*Draws text dynamically*
(See TEXT command.)	
DVIEW	*Dynamically defines parallel or perspective screens*
CA	Select camera angle
CL	Set clipping planes
D	Set distance, turn on perspective
H	Remove hidden lines
OFF	Turn off perspective
PA	Pan drawing
PO	Specify camera and target points
TA	Rotate target point
TW	Twist view
U	Undo
X	Exit
Z	Zoom
DXBIN	*Loads binary files produced by programs such as AutoShade*
DXFIN	*Loads a drawing interchange file*

DXFOUT	*Creates a drawing interchange file for the current drawing*
E	Select specific entities
B	Specify binary file
EDGESURF	*Constructs a Coons surface patch—a polygon mesh bounded on four sides by entities you select*
ELEV	*Controls placement of the current X-Y construction plane on the Z axis*
ELLIPSE	*Draws ellipses*
C	Specify center
R	Rotate ellipse around first axis
I	Draw isometric circle
END	*Saves the drawing and returns you to the Main Menu*
ERASE	*Removes entities from a drawing*
EXPLODE	*Separates a block into its original entities*
EXTEND	*Extends entities to a boundary*
FILES	*Allows you to perform limited system operations while still in AutoCAD*
FILL	*Controls filling of polylines and solids*
ON	Fills solids and wide polylines
OFF	Outlines solids and wide polylines
FILLET	*Trims or extends two entities and places a fillet between them*
P	Fillet polyline
R	Set fillet radius

FILMROLL	_Generates a file used for rendering if you are using AutoShade_
'GRAPHSCR	_Switches a single-screen system from text display to graphics display_
GRID	_Sets up a rectangular array of reference points within the drawing limits_
ON	Turn on grid
OFF	Turn off grid
S	Default grid to snap setting
A	Change X-Y values
number	Set X-Y values
numberX	Set spacing to multiple of snap spacing
HANDLES	_Controls the system variable for unique identifiers for entities_
ON	Assign handles to all entities
DESTROY	Discard all entity handles
HATCH	_Performs hatching_
name	Use hatch pattern "name" from library file
U	Use simple user-defined hatch pattern
?	List names of available hatch patterns

"name" and "U" can be followed by a comma and a
hatch style from the following list:

I	Ignore style
N	Normal style
O	Hatch outermost portion only
?	List available style types
'HELP	_Provides on-line documentation_
HIDE	_Removes hidden lines_

ID	*Returns the coordinates of a point*
IGESIN	*Loads files in the initial graphics exchange standard (IGES) format*
IGESOUT	*Converts current drawing to an IGES format and outputs to a new file*
INSERT	*Inserts previously defined block*
name	Load block file name
name=f	Create block name from file *f*
*name	Retain individual part entities
?	List names of defined blocks
C	Specify corner of scale
XYZ	Readies INSERT for X, Y, and Z scales
ISOPLANE	*Changes the orientation of the crosshairs when working in isometrics*
L	Left plane
R	Right plane
T	Top plane
Return	Toggle to next plane
LAYER	*Creates and modifies layers*
C*c*	Set specified layers to color *c*
F*a,b*	Freeze layers *a* and *b*
L*t*	Set specified layers to linetype *t*
M*a*	Make *a* the current layer
N*a,b*	Create new layers *a* and *b*
ON *a,b*	Turn on layers *a* and *b*
OFF *a,b*	Turn off layers *a* and *b*
S*a*	Set current layer to layer *a*
T*a,b*	Thaw layers *a* and *b*
?	List layers, colors, and linetypes
LIMITS	*Controls drawing size*
2 points	Set lower left and upper right drawing limits

ON	Turn on limits checking
OFF	Turn off limits checking

LINE *Draws a straight line*

Return	Start at end of previous line or arc (as reply to From point:)
C	Close polygon (as reply to To point:)
U	Undo segment (as reply to To point:)

LINETYPE *Creates, loads, and sets linetypes*

?	List available linetypes
C	Create linetype
L	Load linetype
S	Set current entity linetype

LIST *Lists entity information*

LOAD *Loads shape and font files*

?	List loaded shape files

LTSCALE *Changes the scale of linetypes*

MEASURE *Measures a distance, placing points or markers at intervals*

B	Use specified block as marker

MENU *Loads a new menu file for pull-down, screen, tablet, and button menus*

MINSERT *Makes multiple inserts of a block*

name	Load block file name and form a rectangular array
name=f	Create block name from file f and form a rectangular array
?	List names of defined blocks
C	Specify corner of scale
XYZ	Indicate use of X, Y, Z values

MIRROR	*Reflects entities on an axis*
MOVE	*Moves entities in the drawing*
MSLIDE	*Makes a slide of a drawing or part of a drawing*
MULTIPLE	*Repeats another command until canceled*
OFFSET	*Creates a parallel entity*
number	Specify offset distance
T	Specify point through which offset curve will pass
OOPS	*Undoes last group erasure*
ORTHO	*Restricts user to horizontal or vertical movement of the cursor*
ON	Turn on horizontal/vertical constraint
OFF	Turn off horizontal/vertical constraint
OSNAP	*Sets global Object SNAP modes*
CEN	Center of arc or circle
END	Closest endpoint of arc or line
INS	Insertion point of text, block, or shape
INT	Intersection of arc, circle, or line
MID	Midpoint of arc or line
NEA	Point nearest crosshairs on entity
NOD	Node (point)
NON	None; cancel OSNAP mode
PER	Perpendicular to arc, circle, or line
QUA	Quadrant mode of arc or circle
QUI	Quick mode
TAN	Tangent to arc or circle
'PAN	*Allows you to move around in a drawing without changing the zoom factor*

PEDIT (2-D, 3-D)   *Allows you to edit polyline*

C	Close open polyline
D	Decurve polyline
E	Edit vertex
F	Fit curve to polyline (not in 3-D)
J	Join to polyline (not in 3-D)
O	Open polyline
S	Use vertices as frame for spline curve
U	Undo
W	Set uniform width for polyline (not in 3-D)
X	Exit

Options for vertex editing:

B	Set first vertex for break
G	Go
I	Insert new vertex after current vertex
M	Move current vertex
N	Make next vertex current
P	Make previous vertex current
R	Regenerate
S	Set first vertex for straighten
T	Set tangent direction (not in 3-D)
W	Set new width for following segment (not in 3-D)
X	Exit vertex editing; cancel break or straighten

PEDIT (MESH)   *Allows you to edit polygon mesh*

D	Desmooth—restore original
E	Edit vertex
M	Open or close mesh in M direction
N	Open or close mesh in N direction
S	Fit a smooth surface
U	Undo
X	Exit

Options for vertex editing:

D	Move down to previous vertex in M direction
L	Move left to previous vertex in N direction
M	Reposition vertex
N	Move to next vertex
P	Move to previous vertex
R	Move right to next vertex in N direction
RE	Redisplay polygon
U	Move up to next vertex in M direction
X	Exit vertex editing

PLAN *Provides a plan view of the drawing relative to the current UCS, a specified UCS, or the WCS*

C	Display plan view of current UCS
U	Display plan view of specified UCS
W	Display plan view of WCS

PLINE *Draws polylines*

H	Set new half-width
U	Undo last PLINE command
W	Set new line width
Return	Exit

Options for line mode:

A	Change to arc mode
C	Close with straight segment
L	Enter previous segment length

Options for arc mode:

A	Angle
CE	Center point
CL	Close with arc segment
D	Starting direction
L	Length of chord; switch to line mode
R	Radius
S	Second point of three-point arc

PLOT   *Plots a drawing on a pen plotter*

POINT   *Inserts point entities into a drawing*

POLYGON   *Draws polygons*
   E   Specify edge of polygon
   C   Circumscribe
   I   Inscribe

PRPLOT   *Sends a plot to a printer that accepts graphics information*

PURGE   *Cleans up the drawing database by removing unused entities*
   A   Purge all unused, named objects
   B   Purge unused blocks
   LA   Purge unused layers
   LT   Purge unused linetypes
   SH   Purge unused shapes
   ST   Purge unused text styles

QTEXT   *Replaces text with a box*
   ON   Turn on quick-text mode
   OFF   Turn off quick-text mode

QUIT   *Ends the editing session and returns to the Main Menu without saving changes to the drawing*

REDEFINE   *Allows you to restore the standard AutoCAD commands to their original definition*

REDO   *Reverses an UNDO command*

'REDRAW   *Redraws entities on the screen*

'REDRAWALL   *Redraws all viewports at one time*

REGEN   *Regenerates the drawing and redraws the current viewport*

REGENALL   *Regenerates all viewports*

REGENAUTO   *Limits automatic regeneration*
ON   Enables automatic regeneration
OFF   Disables automatic regeneration

RENAME   *Renames entities*
B   Rename block
LA   Rename layer
LT   Rename linetype
S   Rename text style
U   Rename UCS
VI   Rename view
VP   Rename viewport

'RESUME   *Allows for resumption of an interrupted script file*

REVSURF   *Generates a surface of revolution by rotating an outline around an axis*

ROTATE   *Rotates the entities in your drawing*
R   Rotate to referenced angle

RSCRIPT   *Allows for repetition of a script file*

RULESURF   *Creates a ruled surface between two curves, lines, points, arcs, circles, and polylines*

SAVE   *Saves changes made to the drawing, without returning to the Main Menu*

SCALE   *Scales what you have drawn*
R   Scale to referenced length

SCRIPT	*Executes a script file in the Drawing Editor*
SELECT	*Creates a selection set for use in subsequent commands*
'SETVAR	*Accesses system variables*
SH	*Allows a partial shell to the operating system*
SHAPE	*Inserts shapes in the drawing*
?	List shape names
SHELL	*Provides full access to the operating system level*
SKETCH	*Allows freehand drawing*
C	Connect new segments to existing segments
E	Erase
P	Raise or lower pen
Q	Exit sketch mode without saving
R	Save without exiting
X	Save and exit
.	Draw line to current point
SNAP	*Provides an invisible grid that you are locked into*
number	Set alignment
ON	Turn on snap mode
OFF	Turn off snap mode
A	Change X-Y spacing
R	Rotate snap grid
S	Select standard or isometric style
SOLID	*Draws solid rectilinear and triangular areas*

STATUS	*Displays drawing information*
STRETCH	*Changes entities while retaining connections with other entities or points*
STYLE	*Loads text fonts into a drawing*
?	List text styles
TABLET	*Controls use and layout of the tablet*
ON	Turn on tablet mode
OFF	Turn off tablet mode
CAL	Calibrate tablet
CFG	Configure tablet for tablet menus
TABSURF	*Creates a tabulated surface with a path and a direction vector*
TEXT	*Places text in a drawing*
A	Align text between two points
C	Center text horizontally
F	Fit text between two points
M	Center text horizontally and vertically
R	Right-justify text
S	Select text style
'TEXTSCR	*Flips to the text screen on a single-screen system*
TIME	*Keeps track of time spent in a drawing*
D	Display time
ON	Turn on timer
OFF	Turn off timer
R	Reset timer
TRACE	*Draws a line of a specific width*
TRIM	*Trims entities back to a boundary*

U	*Reverses the effect of the most recent command*
UCS	*Defines or modifies the User Coordinate System*
D	Delete specified UCS
E	Use existing entity to define UCS
O	Define new UCS by moving origin of current UCS
P	Make previous UCS current
R	Restore a saved UCS
S	Save current UCS
V	Define new UCS with Z axis parallel to view direction
W	Set current UCS to World Coordinate System
X	Rotate current UCS around X axis
Y	Rotate current UCS around Y axis
Z	Rotate current UCS around Z axis
ZA	Define new UCS with specified origin and positive Z axis
3	Define new UCS with specified origin, positive X axis, and positive Y axis
?	List saved UCSs.
UCSICON	*Controls the User Coordinate System icon that appears at the bottom of drawings in Release 10*
A	Change icon in all viewports
N	Display icon in lower left corner of screen
O	Display icon at origin of current UCS
OFF	Turn off icon
ON	Turn on icon
UNDEFINE	*Defines normal AutoCAD commands to LISP routines*

UNDO		*Reverses the effect of previous commands and provides control over the undo feature*
	number	Undo specified number of commands
	A	Control treatment of menu selections
	B	Undo to previous mark
	C	Toggle undo feature off and on
	E	End undo group
	G	Group commands
	M	Mark a place in undo information
UNITS		*Sets the display format and precision of your drawing units*
'VIEW		*Creates views of zoomed work areas*
	D	Delete specified view
	R	Restore specified view
	S	Save current screen display as view
	W	Make area in window a view
	?	List views
VIEWPORTS *or **VPORTS***		*Controls the number of ports on the screen at a given time*
	D	Delete saved viewport configuration
	J	Join two viewports
	R	Restore saved viewport
	S	Save current viewport
	S1	Display single viewport filling the entire graphics area
	2	Divide current viewport into 2 viewports
	3	Divide current viewport into 3 viewports
	4	Divide current viewport into 4 viewports
	?	List saved viewports
VIEWRES		*Controls AutoCAD's fast regeneration and the resolution of circles and arcs as they are drawn and represented*

VPOINT	*Allows you to see your drawing in three dimensions*
R	Select view using rotation angles
Return	Select view using compass and axes
x,y,z	Specify view point
VSLIDE	*View previously created slides*
file	View slide
★file	Load slide for next VSLIDE
WBLOCK	*Creates blocks that can be used in all drawings*
name	Write file name for block
=	Block name is same as file name
★	Write entire drawing
Return	Write specified block
'ZOOM	*Allows you to magnify or condense parts of the drawing*
number	Zoom by a factor from original scale
numberX	Zoom by a factor from current scale
A	All
C	Specify new center point
D	Dynamic
E	Extents
L	Set new lower left corner
P	Return to previous screen
W	Place window around working area
3DFACE	*Draws three-dimensional flat planes*
I	Make following edge invisible.
3DMESH	*Creates a polygon mesh by specifying the size and vertices*
3DPOLY	*Draws three-dimensional polylines*
C	Close polyline
U	Undo last endpoint
Return	Exit